FROM   STONES

TO STATEHOOD

THE PALESTINIAN UPRISING

PHYLLIS BENNIS

PHOTOGRAPHS BY
NEAL CASSIDY

FOREWORD BY
IBRAHIM ABU LUGHOD

OLIVE
BRANCH
PRESS

An imprint of Interlink Publishing Group, Inc.

First published 1990 by

OLIVE BRANCH PRESS
An Imprint of Interlink Publishing Group, Inc.
99 Seventh Avenue
Brooklyn, New York 11215

Published simultaneously in Great Britain by
Zed Books Ltd.,
57 Caledonian Road,
London N1 9BU

Library of Congress Cataloging-in-Publication Data
Bennis, Phyllis, 1951–
From stones to statehood: the Palestinian uprising / by Phyllis
Bennis; photographs by Neal Cassidy.
p. cm.
Includes index.
ISBN 0–940793–48–2
1. West Bank—History—Palestinian Uprising, 1987– 2. Gaza Strip—History—Palestinian
Uprising, 1987– I. Cassidy, Neal, 1951–.
II. Title.
DS110.W47B42 1989
956.95'3044—dc20   89–15995
                                                                          CIP

British Library Cataloguing in Publication Data
Bennis, Phyllis
From Stones to Statehood.
1. Palestine
I. Title II. Cassidy, Neal
956.94'054

ISBN 0-86232-915-9 pbk
Printed in Hong Kong

Book design by Kamal Boullata

Contents

To Ziya Jihad Fayez Haj-Mohammad
[1983 – 1988]

Acknowledgements

Our trips to the Middle East, and all the work of putting this book together, represented in many ways a collective endeavor. Certainly, our work would not have been possible without the help and support of a number of people and organizations, in the United States, in occupied Palestine, and elsewhere.

The Roots organization in Washington, D.C. provided tremendous assistance for our second trip to the Middle East. The U.S.-Arab Chamber of Commerce, Americans for Middle East Understanding, the staffs of the American-Arab Anti-Discrimination Committee and the Arab-American Institute, the Network for Peace in the Middle East and the Palestine Solidarity Committee all provided help, ideas and moral support.

The Chicago-based DataBase Project on Palestinian Human Rights had extraordinary patience with our constant requests for sources and documentation.

Several individuals helped in getting the book into shape: Joan Andersson, Dr. Naseer Aruri, Dr. Riyad Mansour, Ruth Moushabeck, and Sheila Ryan were among them. Additionally, a number of Palestinian friends, in the United States and in centers of the diaspora, gave generously of their time and encouragement.

The staff of *Frontline* newspaper in some ways made the whole project possible. They encouraged us to expand our articles and photographs to a book, and gave us the support to make it happen. Among them, we must single out the photo team, who worked so hard to get Neal's pictures out across the country when he was shot and after, and editor Ellen Kaiser, who kept Phyllis' sanity intact by long distance telephone during those frantic days while Neal lay in the hospital.

Our families gave us love and support, even when the nature of our work and our constant travels made that difficult.

Kamal Boullata's inspired design, Ibrahim Abu Lughod's thoughtful foreword, and especially the supportive and careful (if sometimes last-minute) editing by Michel Moushabeck, made the book something far better than we could have produced on our own.

And finally, to the people of occupied Palestine, to the people of the intifada, who remain unnamed but very much at the center of our work and of our thoughts, we extend our deepest thanks and admiration. It is through them that we have learned some of the lessons of their heroism and their humility.

P.B. and N.C.

Foreword

In March 1988, at a very important juncture during the Palestinian *intifada*/uprising, Phyllis Bennis and her photographer colleague Neal Cassidy, both of whom had been covering the intifada for *Frontline* newspaper, came to see me, and told me of their plans to go to the West Bank and Gaza. I was delighted, especially when I learned that the purpose of their trip was to put together a book—a book that will allow Palestinians inside the occupied territories to tell the world their story.

Phyllis and Neal's experience, knowledge and understanding of the dynamics of the Palestinian struggle for freedom made them a perfect team for the job. Their courage, enthusiasm and willingness to risk their lives to accomplish their goal made their book an invaluable journal of Palestinian life during the intifada.

Periodically, Phyllis Bennis has provided her readers with a series of brilliant, dispassionate and very careful analyses of the Palestinian encounter with Israel's occupation; they were graphically matched by Neal Cassidy's photographs. Not only were they physically mobile throughout the West Bank and Gaza, but they observed the *intifada* closely, and most importantly, viewed it from the perspective of the Palestinians themselves. They did not depend for information, data and analysis on the handouts of the Israeli army or the so-called "civil" administration.

When the Palestine National Council held its independence meeting in Algiers in November 1988, the intifada was three weeks short of its first anniversary. But by then the major characteristics of the *intifada* had become evident. Israel's failure to contain the *intifada* had become all to clear, despite the incredible political and moral support Israel has been getting from its allies in the Bush administration and in Congress. Only those with a serious understanding of the dynamics of Palestinian history, but with an equally solid understanding of the existential reality of Palestinian society and culture could have appreciated the enormous strength and vitality of the latest manifestation of the Palestinian quest for freedom, independence and sovereignty on their own national soil.

From Stones to Statehood reflects the vitality of the Palestinians as they challenge the occupiers of their land with non-lethal power.

The *intifada* came on the 70th anniversary of the conquest of Palestine by the British imperial forces led by General Allenby. It was British colonialism, with the active collaboration of other European and American powers legitimizing their acts through the League of Nations, that systematically violated the Palestinian right to self-determination. Exercising that right would have led to their national independence and sovereignty in Palestine. The systematic violation of other Third World people's right to self-determination was a common colonial policy. But Palestine was exceptional in that the British prepared the grounds so thoroughly. They facilitated the influx of European Zionist settlers to Palestine and continued to assault the Palestinian national movement. The result was the dismemberment of Palestine, the gradual expulsion of the Palestinians and their dispersion, making possible the establishment of Israel.

Scholars of the Palestinian resistance to British colonialism during the Mandate period are fully cognizant of the periodic rebellions, massive strikes and demonstrations that occurred. These are the weapons that all Third World people used to resist European colonialism. In most cases, following such events, negotiations ensued and independence was wrested from the colonial power. For the Palestinians, the General Strike of 1936 was a prelude to what Palestinians refer to as *al-Thawra al-Arabiyya al-Kubra* (the Great Arab Revolt). But the Palestinians were still the exception to the general trend of decolonization. Instead of achieving independence, they were in 1948 subjected to dispersion, to Israeli settler colonialism and to subordination to Arab governments subservient to European and American domination. Israel's apartheid system made it possible to relegate its Palestinian population to third class status (after European and Oriental Jews) in pre-1967 Israel. Beyond those borders, Israel pursued long range goals of territorial expansion and provided important strategic services to its allies.

Barely 21 years after Israel's occupation of the West Bank and Gaza, and its inhumane treatment of the local population, the Palestinians confronted their occupiers in the *intifada*. Israel should have expected the *intifada*. But blinded by its ideological and historically rooted racism, by its role as a colonial power, and by its close affiliation with the principal western power of the world, Israel and its friends were caught by total surprise when the *intifada* broke out. Its initial response was intended to assure the Israeli public and its supporters in the United States that sufficient use of lethal power would stamp out the uprising in the first two weeks. That stretched to two months and is now in its third year.

Had Israel and its supporters examined somewhat objectively the policies and practices of Israel's occupation of the West Bank and Gaza, they would have known that the Palestinians are as determined to evict that occupation from Palestinian territory as any other people who suffered the brutalities of colonial occupation. Israel should have known that its confiscation of Palestinian lands, estimated at over 60 per cent of the West Bank and Gaza, to make room for new Jewish settlements to facilitate permanent occupation, is not likely to give their occupation a benign face. Its demolishing of thousands of homes of Palestinian citizens, relying on the dubious validity of Britain's notorious defense regulations, deliberately creates homelessness in Palestine just as the world is trying to solve the problem of homelessness. The creation of a large body of cheap labor to do the work which Jewish workers would not do, and certainly at wages no self-respecting Israeli Jew would accept, confirms Israel's determination to generalize an apartheid system.

This system takes on many forms: the imprisonment, detention of thousands of Palestinians, the shooting to death of Palestinians engaged in resisting the occupation as well as those not actively resisting, the severe punishment of Palestinians affirming their cultural identity by singing their national songs, raising their national flag, or affirming that the PLO is their sole representative, and the periodic expulsions of Palestinians from their lifelong homes. It confirms to Palestinians that the occupation aims at their eviction from their national soil and at transforming the entire country into an Israeli Jewish state in which the remaining Palestinian population would be permanently subordinated, exploited and demeaned.

There are a number of crucial questions which *From Stones to Statehood* helps to answer. How could it be that an unarmed population, one-third the size of a powerful occupier that functions militarily as one of the five or six major world powers, has been able to paralyze the functioning of that occupation? How is it that such unarmed resistance on the part of the Palestinians of the West Bank and Gaza, could compel Israel to assign a permanent military occupation force to subdue the local population that is larger than the combined military forces that initially invaded the West Bank and Gaza (more than 100,000)? How has it been possible for a population, whose occupied territory is pockmarked by armed enclaves of racist settlers, not only to resist the occupation, but in the course of two years of *intifada*, to disengage from that occupation and render it illegitimate and obsolete? The answers to these and many similar questions may not be complete and full today. However, our understanding of the uniqueness of the Palestinian struggle today is enormously enhanced by the very perceptive, detailed and matter-of-fact narrative of *From Stones to Statehood*.

It should be evident to the reader of this powerful book that the authors examined the reality with open eyes. They visited the entire area under extremely dangerous circumstances and observed the Israeli army, with all its reputed efficiency and power, trying to smash the Palestinian resistance.

Equally, they saw the enormous power which people display when motivated by the desire to be free and independent.

In their book, Phyllis and Neal are able to depict the occupation. They are able to examine the heroic struggle of men and women, young and old, of ordinary people, of various sectors of society, of villages, in a serious attempt to convey their resilience. But more than that, they are clear in pointing out the irresistible fate of the area – the construction of peace between the antagonists.

The peace that is being constructed by the *intifada* can be witnessed in the rebuilding of Palestinian national institutions, in the emergence of new and model forms of cooperation and discipline that today facilitate the resistance and lay the foundations for durable national independent institutions in the future.

A reader of this powerful and impressively faithful work would conclude that the Israeli occupation in Palestine will be defeated as other forms of colonial occupation have been defeated elsewhere. The beautiful faces of Palestinian men, women and children, so well captured by the photographs that accompany the text, not only point out the human victims in Palestine, but also the bright hopes of a people for a life with dignity and freedom in their own independent state. The author and photographer of this work have clarified what other works have obscured.

Ibrahim Abu-Lughod
Professor of Political Science,
Northwestern University
Member of Palestine National Council

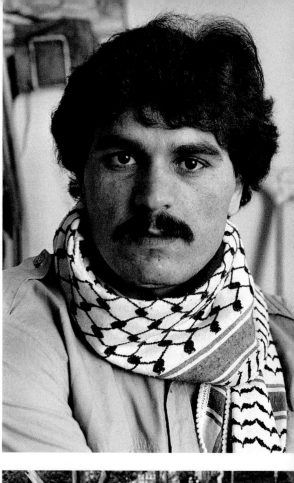

Introduction

When the Palestinian uprising began, before its scope and significance exploded in the consciousness of
the world, I was getting ready to go to
Vietnam for a journalist's conference.
When I returned, in February 1988, the
intifada was two months old. An old
friend called me. "I know you must still
be jet-lagged," he began, "but you've really got to go to the occupied territories
now. This is the time."

I took his call seriously, as I looked
at the stacks of still-unopened mail, and
the piles of still-unanswered phone messages. I knew he was right. I did have to
go.

I had never been to the Middle East
before, although I had been involved
with the issue for a long time. When the
Vietnam war ended, I had looked for a
new direction for my political work, and
became involved with the Middle East
and the question of Palestine. I had been
writing and doing radio commentary on
the issue since the late 1970s.

Some people I knew said it was
probably an inevitable shift for a Jewish
Zionist youth group leader-turned-rebel. I
see it differently; I think I was more
fortunate than most, because I made contact with people who could teach me,
and alert me to the injustices going on in
that part of the world, at a time when the
United States anti-war movement was
still relatively ignorant about the Middle
East. Now, I knew I had to go to see for
myself.

Neal Cassidy, a friend and longtime
Frontline photographer, didn't need

much persuading to join me. Neal had worked for many years as an activist-photographer, and his skills and courage would prove crucial to our work.

We left for our first trip just a few weeks later. During our stay in the West Bank and Gaza, in the spring of 1988, we managed to see more of the intifada, to meet more people, and to have more opportunities for discussion, than we had expected.

After we arrived there, we spent two days in Gaza, staying in a new friend's home, sleeping, or trying to sleep, through the noise of military patrols in the streets of Khan Yunis camp. We were at Al-Ittihad Hospital in Nablus on April 6 when the Palestinian dead were brought from Beita, killed by an Israeli settler who then killed one of his young Israeli charges. We were held at the Beita roadblock by soldiers trying to prevent our return to Jerusalem.

Neal and I did not travel to the West Bank and Gaza as neutral observers. We have tried, I think successfully, to be honest in what we report; but that is not the same as being neutral. So, like any book worth reading about the Middle East, our book is partisan. Being partisan does not allow one to fail in honesty, to fail to tell the truth. But it does mean choosing the story that one will tell, and being honest in what has been left out.

During our stay inside occupied Palestine, we were drawn to the battles taking place daily in the streets. We tried to delve into their roots, to look beyond the immediate clashes to discover what was behind the young, unarmed Palestinians daily defying Israel's military might. We learned something else indeed was going on behind this compelling scene.

We had come to the West Bank and Gaza at a moment of transition in the intifada. The immediate resistance, the street-level confrontations between soldiers and the Palestinian population, while continuing, no longer formed the central core of the uprising.

The intifada was no longer just a series of spontaneous acts of resistance; an entire occupied population was transforming itself into a mobilized, conscious state-in-formation. Popular institutions, for governing, for organizing economic life, for social mobilization, were exploding throughout the territories. The creation of these alternative institutions, this new state structure, intersected with the street-level resistance to the occupation. This was the new Palestine. This was what we returned for.

In the fall of 1988, we returned to follow this mostly-invisible, mostly-hidden story. There was a bigger story than what people were seeing on the 20-second television sound bites each night. We knew there was a much fuller story that needed to be told, and pictures that needed to be shown.

This second, and much longer trip, was interrupted prematurely, when Neal was shot by an Israeli soldier. Photographing a patrol in the casbah, or Old City, of Nablus on October 18, an Israeli Defense Force rifleman took aim and shot him in the leg with a plastic bullet.

Neal was lucky, relatively — the soldier was far enough away that the bullet did not do permanent damage. It was removed by surgeons at the Palestinian Al-Ittihad Hospital in Nablus, and healed cleanly. But Neal Cassidy was now the first foreign journalist (and an American at that!) to be shot during the intifada — it was news. He refused an Israeli army commander's request (delivered with machine guns in hand by a patrol of a dozen or so soldiers crowding into his hospital room within an hour after surgery) to be moved from Al-Ittihad to an Israeli hospital. As a result, during his days in the hospitals, first Al-Ittihad and then at Al-Makassad Hospital in Jerusalem, Neal was treated as a popular hero, and spent hours studying Arabic with the *shebab*, the young men hospitalized with their own intifada injuries.

After a few days back in the U.S., mostly for further recuperation, and so Neal and I could reassure our worried families that we really were all right, we headed back to the Middle East. This time, we didn't go directly to the West Bank.

Instead, we travelled to Algiers, where the Palestinian parliament-in-exile, the Palestine National Council, was convening on November 15 in special session. We joined hundreds of Palestinians from around the world, and hundreds more international journalists, in witnessing the birth of the new State of Palestine, to hear the Declaration of Independence read by PLO Chairman Yasir Arafat.

When we arrived in Jerusalem after the PNC, the first anniversary of the uprising was almost at hand. The Israelis knew that those would be days of tremendous nation-wide mobilization. They announced a four-day-long curfew for virtually all of the West Bank and Gaza far in advance of the anniversary itself.

Our last days in occupied Palestine were spent in a frenzy of work to get all the interviews, all the pictures, all the impressions we could gather to take back with us. *From Stones to Statehood* is the result.

I should perhaps add a note here about the use of names; there aren't very many in the book. The people we spent time with, whether in hours of interviews or on special trips to photograph demonstrations; whether intifada activists or simply Palestinians who welcomed us as guests in their homes — all of them could face serious jeopardy if their identities were to be exposed. So except for a few individuals, who are already public figures, we have chosen not to identify our sources by name, only by their role in the intifada, or perhaps by where they live.

This book tells one story, shows one side: that of the Palestinians fighting to reclaim their rights to nationhood in their ancient land. As much as possible, I have told their story in the words of the Palestinians' themselves.

Certainly, there are other stories that should be told. There are Israeli Jews who fight courageously for peace, and who have paid a bitter price in isolation and attack. But this is not their story. There are other Israelis, who fight hard against peace, against tolerance, against justice; many of them live in settlements in the Palestinian lands of the West Bank and Gaza, others prowl the halls of the Knesset. But this is not their story either.

This is only one story, and it is an unfinished story, for the State of Palestine has not yet been fully born. The intifada is continuing, and has become a way of life for an entire people. Certainly, there will be hard times ahead, there will be setbacks and defeats, but through the labor pains of this intifada, the 'terrible beauty' of Palestinian independence, of nationhood, is now being born.

Phyllis Bennis
New York, 1990

1. The Occupation, The Uprising

On December 8, 1987, near the densely crowded checkpoint at the entrance to the occupied Gaza Strip, an incident occurred. It involved an Israeli truck — some say an army truck — that swerved, and struck and killed four Palestinians: a doctor, an engineer and two workers. Some say it was deliberate. What makes this incident different from the hundreds, perhaps thousands, of similar incidents during the 20 years of Israeli occupation was its outcome.

The incident was different, this time, because it sparked an uprising that swept across the Gaza Strip, jumped like a roaring forest fire across Israeli territory to the occupied West Bank, and set into motion a blaze of nationalist resistance that has not yet been extinguished.

The uprising ignited in a specific time and a specific place. The time was now, only now, at the confluence of years of smoldering and waiting, and the immediate spark of the moment's crisis.

In some ways, the real surprise was not that the uprising began, but that it did not begin earlier. The occupation, after all, had been going on for more than 20 years. The denial of national rights, the disorientation of Palestinians being made refugees in their own land, the constant repression, all led to widespread despair — and for many living under Israeli military control, to passivity.

The Palestinians living in the West Bank and Gaza are a young community; more than half the population grew up knowing nothing but Israeli occupation. Only now, has the intifada brought new hope for challenging the occupation; only now, especially since the Declaration of an independent State of Palestine on November 15, 1988, is there a glimmer of what a Palestine free from occupation could look like.

One community leader in Beit Sahour, near Bethlehem, said "Palestine has become the intifada. And the intifada is transforming Palestine."

But however the uprising began, if it had been strictly spontaneous, it would have collapsed in just a few weeks. The ferocity of Israel's counter-attack left little hope for an ad-libbed resistance movement.

But this resistance was not ad-libbed. A popular committee representative from the small northern village of Qabatiya described how "the intifada was spontaneous at first. But after about one month, our earlier organizing efforts took root, and gained control of the political motion of the intifada. That is what allowed the uprising to continue."

Existing grass-roots organizations inside occupied Palestine quickly mobilized their resources to respond to the new challenges posed every day. Their leaders met to assess, and try to answer, the needs of the population as institutions of the occupation authority crumbled.

One El Bireh leader described how "the reasons for the intifada are both objective and subjective. The objective reason, of course, is the 21 years of occupation, of repression. The subjective side is the Palestinian resistance movement we have built over those same 21 years, increasing the participation of every sector of society. It was the accumulation of those objective and subjective factors together that created the intifada. Nothing is spontaneous here any more."

At the same time, the clandestine local branches of the PLO's main constituent groups, already well positioned inside the broader local organizations,

emerged to play a more public role. Public, that is, as integral and acknowledged parts of the emerging infrastructure of the new Palestinian community life. The individual leaders of these movements collectively soon joined with representatives of the local organizations to form the Unified National Leadership of the Uprising (UNLU).

The individuals comprising the UNLU, and its quickly created neighborhood, district, city, and regional branches, remained secret. A member of the popular committee (the local branch of the UNLU) in Qabatiya, speaking during the uprising's eighth month, said "I think the UNLU members are all in prison, I don't think they're outside. But they still are leading us, and communication with them was never broken, even during the 42 days that our village was under siege by the soldiers."

The UNLU itself remains underground. Despite frequent Israeli claims of having destroyed the leadership core, UNLU has been consistently visible through its regular communiques. Those numbered leaflets, appearing suddenly on street corners throughout the West Bank and Gaza about every two weeks, identify the new stages of the uprising, and coordinate the various aspects of resistance. Each leaflet, eagerly awaited, outlines the specific tasks for each day of the coming period. Which are the days for complete commercial strikes, which to protest the condition of prisoners in administrative detention, which to work on the land, which to highlight women's roles in the uprising, which to confront the occupation's military forces, which to spend in commemorating the legacy of the intifada's martyrs.

From the beginning, the UNLU was led by representatives of the four parties of what many Palestinians call the PLO's "consensus bloc": Chairman Yasir Arafat's mainstream Al-Fatah, the largest and most influential faction within the

PLO, the Popular and Democratic Fronts for the Liberation of Palestine, and the Palestine Communist Party. In Gaza, where the influence of Islam is stronger, the regional UNLU included representatives of Islamic Jihad (a Palestinian-based organization unrelated to the Iranian-backed Lebanese fundamentalist group of the same name).

The composition of the UNLU made possible two key links in sustaining the uprising. First, the connection between the PLO's underground political organizations and the community associations ensured a leadership with both a local understanding of the conditions inside the occupied territories, and the long-range vision and widespread credibility of the liberation movement. Second, the local branches of the PLO's organizations remained in constant contact with their exiled national leadership. This resulted in a far-reaching democratization of PLO decision-making, and especially a new priority inside the PLO given to the role and opinions of those Palestinians living under occupation.

"We have to say," an activist from one of the women's committees in Ramallah said, "that the Unified Leadership, in whose name the Calls have been issued, is the voice of the PLO in the West Bank and Gaza, in all the occupied land. Really, we are not disconnected from the PLO, we are one people outside and inside the territories. We have one aim, and the PLO is our representative. . . . Whether we talk about the grassroots committees or the leadership, the UNLU, they are actually representing groups which are part of the PLO. We are one, and the PLO is our sole representative, and they fulfill our aspirations."

It is not surprising that the PLO's role should be such a central one. While Palestinians have recognized the organization as their sole legitimate representative for more than 20 years, the five years leading up to the intifada brought about a heightened level of PLO involvement in the West Bank and Gaza. It began in 1982, when the PLO was forced to leave Lebanon as the culmination of Israel's invasion. The evacuation followed the siege of Beirut, in which the PLO, allied with Lebanese resistance fighters, managed to hold off the Israeli army for more than 100 days.

On the ship to their new home-in-exile in Tunis, PLO leaders acknowledged the fact that a strategy relying on centers of the Palestinian diaspora to lead the fight for independence had not achieved its aims. Instead, a new approach galvanized long-standing PLO commitments to support organizing efforts inside occupied Palestine. Groups like the Shabiba youth movement gained new vitality. The four women's organizations, linked to the main PLO factions, grew in size and influence. Trade unions, already among the largest of Palestinian community organizations, grew in influence, and economic issues have increasingly merged with nationalist demands. Small-scale agricultural cooperatives and popular health organizations took shape to offer alternatives to relying on Israeli goods and services.

So the involvement of the PLO in what were — and remain — truly local, grassroots organizations, has been a feature of Palestinian life for years. Rather than a conflict, that intersection has resulted in Palestinians creating institutions that can answer immediate needs with long-range, visionary projects that function as centers of national resistance as well as providing social services.

In El Bireh, a small town alongside Ramallah, a popular committee leader said, "the political progress of the UNLU is a true example of Palestinian aims: to achieve our right to return to our land, our national self-determination, and our independent state. The UNLU now is the organizational structure of our national life, including mobilizing support among all the people for those goals. That mobilization work is part of the services provided by the UNLU to the rest of us. And the role and significance of UNLU is enhanced as it creates even stronger national unity, and takes us from one stage of the uprising to the next."

The grassroots organizations are of two distinct but inter-related types. Some form the basis for mobilizing and energizing Palestinians on the basis of social factors. Thus the women's associations, trade unions, student and professional groups, farmers' and merchants' organizations all play a critical role in involving those sectors in the uprising.

Other groups, some with a history many years older than the intifada, function as alternative social service organizations, providing for food production and distribution, health needs, financial assistance and education on a society-wide basis. Some form the basis for an increasingly independent Palestinian economy — including the merchants' organizations that determine the character of the intifada's commercial strikes, agricultural co-operatives, trade unions forging new relations with Palestinian factory owners.

The role of these new institutions grows as the status and power of the occupation authorities weaken. The astonishing multiplicity and consolidation of these popular organizations, a key part of the uprising's strategy, set the conditions for a kind of dual power in the West Bank and Gaza, in which Palestinian national institutions contend directly with the military-controlled structures of Israeli occupation.

According to a women's association leader, "this dual power is what we are aiming at with the uprising, to create a gap between the Palestinians under occupation and the Israeli authorities. For the last 20 years, Israel was able to create this connection between the Palestinian population and the occupation authority. There is the economic link, for example.

We have been completely dependent on the Israeli economy. We were without an infrastructure of our own, or an economy, or a state. We had nothing, so we had to be dependent on their economy. And many people were really collaborating with them. Now what the uprising is doing is disconnecting, creating a complete disconnection, by going to the policemen, asking them to resign, asking people not to pay taxes, all these things. . . . You can feel that a Palestinian authority has somehow been created during this uprising. You can feel it in the neighborhood committees, where everybody in a neighborhood gets together, to form a guard committee, agricultural committee, food storage, education, sort of a small government in the street. And really, the Israelis cannot do anything about it."

Taken together, the two kinds of popular institutions weave a tight fabric of Palestinian resistance, self-reliance, and an extraordinary level of unity, across class, sex, geographic, occupational, and age lines. When joined with the PLO's vision for the creation of an independent Palestine, the result is the nascent apparatus of a state. The popularly chosen leadership of the neighborhood, city, and national institutions of the intifada, the emerging structures for governing a new society, coalesce in the Unified National Leadership of the Uprising.

A women's association leader explained in Jerusalem that "the reason people follow the UNLU has to do with the fact that the leadership is not just coming down from above. It's not just giving orders to people, that some might choose to follow and some choose not to. The leadership really comes from inside the people themselves, reflecting the people's own aspirations. This is because of the work of the popular committees. You can feel what the wants of the people are, what their needs are. The Calls reflect things people really want to do, not something they cannot do, something out of reach. When the UNLU calls for a general strike, not one shop is open, not one person walks on the street. . . . We see an uprising now that is ongoing, escalating. It involves all sectors of people now, all classes. We see the shopkeepers involved. We see the workers involved — it's not just a student revolution. The UNLU and the committees are working with the people to organize their lives in a new way, to make their lives ready for this uprising."

The El Bireh leader said in October 1988 that "the UNLU has adopted a strategic slogan — independence and freedom — for the intifada. For this stage, we accept the interim demands identified in the early leaflets, including return of the deportees, release of political prisoners and detainees, withdrawal of the army from the territories, and others.

"The next stage will be one of national disobedience — a complete boycott of the occupation authorities. We don't view that as passive. It will include confrontations with the army and people will go to work in national [Palestinian-owned] factories. It would not mean just staying home. National disobedience will be side by side with continuing and escalating resistance to occupation. Now, the popular committees are an alternative to the occupation authorities. How soon we can reach the stage of national disobedience depends on the work of the popular committees. They strive to make people self-reliant by attempting to organize all of society sector by sector.

"To move toward the next stages, even just to endure, total unity is required. Our assessment is that a high level of unity exists now, because of the intifada. It doesn't matter what faction you belong to or what your political views are — the popular committees are achieving their purpose of building that unity."

25

2. The People

"We are creating a different kind of person now," the village leader in Beit Sahour mused one day, "even as we build the uprising. In the past, sometimes there was selfishness, or a lack of cooperation. People wanted to build their own castle, alone, to say 'I want my wife, my children, to be better off.' Now it's different, now people are cooperating. We all have the same feelings toward the future, because we had the same problems in the past. We share the same dreams now."

Those shared dreams are part of the changes going on inside Palestinian society as a result of the uprising. The outside world, watching the intifada through a prism of media-defined headlines, sees mostly the most direct forms of resistance against the occupying army: Palestinian children throwing stones at well-armed Israeli troops.

And certainly that stone-throwing has been, and remains, a critical component of this multifaceted intifada. But the children of the stones are part of a larger process as well. Their stones and slingshots have become catalysts for far-reaching changes within Palestinian life.

The Arabic root for "intifada," the word "nafada," focuses more on the internal aspects of the process than on its impact on the external world — Palestinian scholar Shukri Abed writes that nafada means to shudder or tremble, to shake off or shake out, to recover or jump to one's feet.

Knowing the importance of what something is called to determine how it is

27

viewed, Palestinians chose "uprising" as the closest English equivalent for intifada. And though it pinpoints direct resistance to Israeli occupation as the key characteristic, "uprising" still misses some of the layers of meaning. In part, this might be attributable to the rich complexity of Arabic compared to the more precise and linear English. But whatever word is used, the internal consequences of the intifada within Palestinian public and private life, may well prove to be as revolutionary and long-lasting as its task of ending the occupation. The "shaking off" of passivity, of old ideas constrained by feudal traditions, or the "jumping to their feet" of newly mobilized sectors of society, all are part of the ongoing intifada.

The cultural changes began to emerge as early as the first months of the uprising. The visible leadership role of many Palestinian women directly challenged — although it did not yet entirely end — the legacy of women being kept at home and out of public life. The popularity of Arabic and Western pop music declined. It was replaced by smuggled in and widely distributed cassettes of nationalist and revolutionary "intifada music." Wedding customs began to change, as once-extravagant celebrations were pared down to more modest family-based affairs, and traditional lavish dowries were supplanted by collections of money to support the uprising. The traditional three-day mourning period has been recast for martyrs of the intifada: from days of prayer and keening, to three-day strikes with shuttered shops and soldiers challenged, with funeral processions transformed into protest marches.

A popular committee leader in Qabatiya described how "social organization here used to be based on tribal and clan affiliation, with status determined by family ties. Now it is based on our new democracy, with respect based on how much each person participates. We are changing our culture and consciousness. Building a new culture is part of building a new state. There is a status imposed on us by the occupation — either you have to deal with it or you are lost. People used to be afraid to discuss politics because of the military authorities — now no one cares about them. In the early days of the intifada the children would run away crying when they heard shooting; now even the pigeons are accustomed to the shots."

A young Qabatiya man, after hiding from the Israeli military for five months, was finally caught and spent six months in administrative detention at the Ansar III prison in the Negev desert. When released he was married in a small family ceremony three weeks later. The next morning, the young man spoke, his new bride at his side, with her hands still ritually henna-stained and dressed in her wedding gold. "The intifada has united people. We have easier relations now between people, and all our people are stronger."

In Geneva, on the night of Yasir Arafat's address to the United Nations, Akram Haniyeh reflected on the impact of the uprising on Palestinian society. A noted journalist and short story writer, Haniyeh was expelled from his birthplace in the West Bank in 1986. He is now part of the PLO's committee on the occupied territories.

"No one should be surprised by the intifada," Haniyeh told me, "except we were all surprised by our people's ability to sacrifice. The intifada has taught all of us. It has educated our people. The nida'at [communiques of the UNLU] are not an invention of the national movement, their outcome comes from the people. The intifada has built a new model, something entirely new to the international heritage of revolution. The people have revolutionary initiative now. They have the ability to face the new needs of the uprising as those needs escalate."

THE WOMEN

How to provide for these "escalating new needs" as the society-wide resistance tears down the old, already inadequate institutions, became, within the first months of the uprising, a critical question for the Palestinians.

Military-imposed curfews and sieges become routine; how to feed an entire village or refugee camp during a 24-hours-a-day shoot-to-kill curfew? What Defense Minister Rabin defined as "might, force and beatings" and "breaking their bones" becomes official Israeli policy; how to provide medical care when the existing government and private hospitals are already insufficient and doctors are beaten by soldiers or turned away at roadblocks? Virtually all schools are closed February 3rd, in the second month of the intifada; how to provide some learning for a generation of Palestinian children faced with losing an entire year of education?

From the beginning, responsibility for coming up with solutions to these and other complex problems, was largely shouldered by the women. Organized on neighborhood, district, city-wide, regional and national levels, the women's committees had for years played a critical role in both the nationalist movement and the separate, but integrally related, efforts to involve Palestinian women in social and political life. Such efforts were traditionally held back by generations of male-dominated feudal customs.

A woman from the Ramallah branch of the Union of Palestinian Women's Committees said "the role of women has changed a lot in the course of this uprising. Palestinian women have been very involved in all aspects of the resistance: from participating in demonstrations, throwing stones, to taking care of what we now call 'being ready' for the national disobedience stage. That means taking care of the work at home, being ready in their houses with stored food, with supplies. . . . They are getting used to this idea of a home economy; women are taking a major role here too. Their lives in general have been hit badly by the Israelis. Women have been shot in the streets, they have been gassed, they have miscarried because of the teargas, they have been imprisoned under administrative detention. So you can feel that there's a big change in the role of women during this uprising, in their day-to-day lives, and in their role in the whole revolution and the Palestinian cause."

Each of the four women's organizations runs kindergartens and child care centers; conducts literacy and skills classes; helps to create and support agricultural and food processing cooperatives; and maintains a wide variety of discussion and support groups, and other activities women in Western countries generally define as "consciousness raising." These activities began years before the intifada began, and have not stopped even under the vastly broadened new demands made on the organizations. In fact, far more women are involved in these long-standing activities than at any time before the uprising.

Women's organizations have also been historically responsible for charitable work. One of the largest charities, the Society of In'ash el-Usra, is run by a remarkable woman in her 60s, Samiha Khalil. Khalil lived in Gaza refugee camps from 1948–52, after her family was expelled from their home in Majdel, near Ramle. She formed the society in 1965, when she returned to Palestine after years in Jordan. She is a member of the Palestine National Council, the Palestinians' parliament-in-exile, but has consistently been denied permission by the Israelis to leave the West Bank to attend meetings of the PNC.

"In'ash el-Usra was organized three months before Al-Fatah was formed,"

Khalil said. "It has a long history. Right now only our kindergarten, nursery and children's home have been allowed to remain open. We had a training center, for girls to learn hairdressing and business skills, a dental office — but the Israelis closed them all down [in response to the intifada]. They closed all our money-making enterprises — the dress factory, our biscuit factory. You can still smell the sweet fragrance from the baking through the locked gate. But we still have 1,800 families who get help from In'ash el-Usra; 108 are completely supported by our Society."

"Since 1917," Khalil explained, "Palestine has been under occupation — we never had permission to defend our land. There have been thousands of intifadas, but this one has lasted much longer. Every day, every hour the authorities do bad things — they cut down trees full of fruit, they take our lands. They come here [to the West Bank] and build settlements even though they still have much more land inside the 1967 borders. It proves that they don't want peace, they are liars."

"During the intifada, our society is helping four times the number of people as before. On the first days of the month, 200 to 300 families come here for assistance. Another 1,000 families, whose sons or supporters are in administrative detention, get assistance too. They get money and help with school expenses. Before the uprising, our expenses here were $210,000 per month and we covered 85% of it by our own enterprises. The biscuit factory alone made 6,000 JDs [Jordan dinars — about $18,000] profit. Now both the biscuit factory and the dress factory have been closed.

"We have 152 kids, ages three to 16, boarding at our children's center. Some are orphans, others' fathers were killed. Many are from families of long-term prisoners who can't take care of the kids. . . . We are moving toward an in-dependent state, so we help the families not only with money, but towards self-sufficiency. We bought rabbit and chicken supplies and opened a training center, but it was closed down. In the villages we have sewing and pottery classes. The society now sells the embroidery from 5,000 women — three times the number as before. We also make prisoner clothes to be donated through the Red Cross.

"After independence, the role of our society will be to help build our new state."

But the pre-intifada tasks and charitable work of the women's organizations are only a small part of what must be done during the uprising. The women take primary responsibility for organizing increased food production in preparation for long-term sieges where the Israeli soldiers prevent anyone from entering or leaving the village or camp. Here certain feudal traditions help; the women of every household are accustomed to storing large amounts of basic foodstuffs. Medical care, provided by the various Palestinian medical organizations, is coordinated by the women's associations: They conduct first-aid training, mobilize blood donations and blood-typing campaigns, and smuggle medical personnel into closed areas to treat the wounded. Popular education, the alternative (and illegal) classes designed to circumvent the forced closing of the schools, is implemented by separate neighborhood committees, but coordinated by the women's groups.

The political views of the four main Palestinian women's associations roughly parallel those of the four organizations of the PLO's "consensus bloc." But while there may be differences on some long-range questions, there is firm unity on the need to mobilize all women in support of the intifada, the PLO and an independent Palestinian state. In fact, the emerging unity among the women's groups has been both an example to and a reflection of the growing unity within the PLO itself.

A women's demonstration at the Al-Aqsa Mosque in Jerusalem's Old City was jointly sponsored by the four organizations on October 10, 1988. Filtering into the large square surrounding the mosque in twos and threes, the women gathered quietly near one wall. Muffled by the chants calling the faithful to prayer, the women finished discussing their demands. One of the women secretly slipped me the hand-written list on a much-folded piece of paper under the eyes of surrounding Israeli soldiers, who had apparently been tipped off to the women's plans.

The demands were: "1) End the repressive Israeli measures against our Palestinian people. 2) Close the military detention centers and release all Palestinian political and administrative detainees. 3) Immediately open all schools and educational institutions to practice our legitimate right of education. 4) Immediate Israeli withdrawal from the occupied land, and allow for temporary international supervision until Palestinians achieve our national and legitimate rights of return, self-determination, and an independent Palestinian state under the leadership of the sole and legitimate representative, the PLO."

In the fetid, muddy Jabaliya refugee camp in the Gaza Strip, activists from the Palestinian Working Women's Committee discussed their work.

"Our Committee was established in 1980, and our work since then focused on problems caused by the Israelis. We used to hold general meetings for women in the camp. Then the military started preventing our projects, so we became more active.

"Now, during the intifada we visit the martyrs' families here in the camp. We're working with the other women's organizations to plan demonstrations for International Women's Day. We also work with the Red Crescent Society to provide medical care and organize blood donation drives. We held marches in the camp to celebrate Children's Day.

"Women face many difficulties in the intifada. Our committee is trying to organize projects for family-based economy, lectures, etc., but there are many restrictions. The strikes and curfews create problems for our organizing. We try to organize visits by quarters — family visits, house visits, to discuss new circumstances, developments in the uprising, but there are too many days of curfew. It means that we can't meet all together, not even our leadership — but we still have ways to share ideas about the intifada."

In the autumn of the uprising's first year, a meeting of the district coordinating committee was held for representatives of the neighborhood branches of one of the women's committees in the Ramallah-El Bireh area. Nine women were present, ranging in age from 18 to mid-40s. Seven were in blue jeans, one in a long Muslim gown and headscarf, and the eldest in a traditional embroidered Palestinian dress.

The meeting began with a discussion of political events — the upcoming Israeli elections, the PLO's plans to convene a meeting of the Palestine National Council. Following the update, an educational presentation on the role of women in Palestinian society from 1900–1967 led to a spirited discussion of the women's movements, charitable organizations, and the political and nationalist roles of Palestinian women in the early years.

The business portion of the meeting started with recruiting problems. "Our relations with new supporters of the committee are very good," one local leader said. "But there are lots of problems, especially now during the intifada. Our recruiting is slow." A member of the district committee said later that "membership is taken very seriously by the committee. A supporter is not approached to become a full member until she can fulfill all the work asked of members. She must be politically aware and willing to work in one of our sub-committees."

Each local representative reported on the work done in her own neighborhood, each of which develops its own plan. The plans are based on some combination of preparing strike days and demonstrations against the occupation, coordinating medical services, organizational and cultural work within the committee, arranging popular education classes for the children, and economic work, including building small-scale cooperatives.

"We have to recognize the differences between our neighborhoods," one woman said after the meeting. "But all the neighborhoods together cooperate in popular education and things like that. The broader committee leadership visits our groups, including supporters and sympathizers, for fuller discussions. But it's a problem because meetings take so much time. I barely have time to feed the kids lunch."

In the final part of the meeting, the women discussed what they would read to prepare for the educational presentation at the next meeting. They then discussed the meeting itself, evaluating what had been accomplished.

A long-standing problem revolved around the time of the meeting. There was no easy time for nine women, most with children and households to look after, to get together. "Let's try to have a discussion about the time of the meeting without having a revolt on our hands," the chair pleaded.

Another problem was created by the children themselves. Five or six of the younger ones were at the meeting, playing in an adjoining room. Periodically one or another would cry, fight, or want her or his mother, and, not surprisingly, the women all had different views on how to respond. "I'm bothered by my child's crying more than you are," one woman said, "I have to get up every time. I know it bothers you, but what can I do?" The women discussed the general problem of inadequate child care, and the reality that now, during the uprising, they tended to want to indulge their children however they could in matters of allowing noise, giving attention etc. "The kids suffer so much every day from the intifada," one woman said, "that many mothers are reluctant to deny them anything ."

The problem of child care reflects the degree to which women's roles in Palestinian society are still affected by long-standing, male-dominated traditions. Despite the astonishing advances of women to positions of leadership in the uprising's popular organizations and in the daily resistance to occupation, the women are still expected to maintain full responsibility for taking care of the children, for buying food and feeding the entire family, for cleaning the house. So a woman who spends a morning organizing a demonstration, an afternoon teaching first aid classes to village girls, and the evening discussing how to expand the local chicken cooperatives, still must run home to feed and care for her house and family.

There is a visible difference between women activists and other women in camps or villages, in the role they play in household life. While even the most active women leaders are usually expected to maintain full responsibility for household work, the activists participate as well in political discussions with outsiders; other women often do not.

In the Khan Yunis refugee camp in the Gaza Strip, a dozen or so young people gathered in early April to discuss the uprising with us. They were all men. The discussion lasted for several hours, during

which the women of the house were glimpsed only briefly, silently, as they brought endless trays of coffee and tea, prepared and served dinner, and swept up the men's carelessly thrown cigarette butts.

Shortly before 10 p.m., when the army's shoot-to-kill curfew went into effect, the visiting young men left, and we prepared to spend the night with the Khan Yunis family. Neal was taken to a room usually occupied by one of the brothers in the family; another brother also had his own room, and a third shared his with his wife and small child. I slept with the grandmother, mother, three sisters and small granddaughter of the family in one room on wall-to-wall mattresses. The men went to sleep first, the women about an hour later, only after cleaning up from dinner. The women were awake by 5:00 a.m., to bake the bread for the household since the camp's bakeries had been shut down during the curfew. The women swept and washed the floors and courtyard, and had the fresh bread and a lavish breakfast ready for the men when they got up at 7:30.

I asked a doctor from one of the medical committees' mobile clinics why virtually all his patients that day in the small village in the Jordan Valley were women and children. He answered that Palestinian men are in fact generally healthier than the women. "Sure, the men work hard and their lives are filled with stress," he said. "But at least when they go home they can sit back and relax because the women take care of them. For the women, there is no leisure, none at all."

The Palestinian birth rate, already high, has risen steeply during the intifada. While this is generally a matter of choice, not coercion — women speak with pride of raising many children to help in the fight for independence — the impact of the soaring birth rate further exacerbates the inequality of men's and women's lives.

Many women spoke of the lessons they had learned from Algeria, where progress toward women's equality during the fight against the French, faded quickly after independence. "We will not be like the Algerian women who went back to their houses after the revolution," said a woman in Jabaliya camp. "Our revolution will continue after the establishment of our independent state. We will continue our struggle for equality."

"It's important to mobilize women, especially now for the intifada," a representative of the Women's Committee for Social Work said. "We have to go to all the organizations, build new committees and attend to women's social needs. We have to push women to participate in demonstrations and committees. Some husbands are supportive, but some are not. We visit the women whose husbands object, and try to talk to the men, to convince them to allow their wives to participate. The intifada has forced more women to go out and participate."

The uprising is changing the women's own views of the connection between the mobilizing of women as women, and opposing the occupation. "Before the intifada we focused on building our women's unions," an activist from the Women's Action Committee in Dheisha refugee camp said. "We worked for improving women's situation in general, as well as the political situation.

"During the intifada, the situation is different. We work harder than before. Now our struggle as women fighting against the occupation is close to that of men. So we have a new role — to help the men, to work together in all ways. One example is the work of women in demonstrations here in Dheisha. Most of the women can't throw stones as well as the men, so we carry the stones close to the men. We build blockades, watch for

soldiers, and pull arrested prisoners away from the soldiers. During the curfews, men can't walk around at all — but women can a little easier, to go and get food."

A young girl from the committee, maybe 15 years old, with a bandaged skull, spoke quietly. "Four days ago, a young man was killed here in Dheisha camp," she said. "The people wanted to take his body to the cemetery, but soldiers surrounded the camp and started pushing people. The *shebab* [the youth of the camp] took his body from the hospital, and tried to get it out of the camp. The soldiers tried to stop them, and beat some girls while the *shebab* threw stones."

When the girl tried to help the *shebab*, the soldiers saw her. One fired directly at her head, from just two meters away. By luck, the bullet only grazed her skull. "I fell down, dizzy; I was bleeding," she continued. "I thought I was going to die. All I could think about was the youth — I was afraid, and I took what I thought was my last look at the young men from Dheisha who were fighting the soldiers. But I was lucky and now it feels like it's a new life for me."

The girl's mother didn't know immediately that her daughter had been shot. "When I found out, my heart boiled," she said. "I wanted to kill. I didn't know which hospital she was in. I finally found her in Al-Hussein Hospital and saw she would be all right."

Will you stop her from going out to confront the soldiers now? "Why would I forbid her to go out now?" the mother answered. "If my daughter is injured, they still can't stop our struggle. Her injury was easy, so we are really very happy. I have a new life for my daughter."

●

THE WORKERS
AND TRADE UNIONS

"The intifada has meant empowerment for Palestinian workers. As a result, there has been a rise in worker militancy on the local level. Confronting the occupation also means looking at the internal economic situation they face. The increased demand for national products [from Palestinian-owned factories], combined with high unemployment in the West Bank and Gaza, leads some Palestinian employers to exploit workers. We are trying for equality of sacrifice."

That assessment, from Marty Rosenbluth, an American researcher at Al-Haq/Law in the Service of Man, touches on the extraordinary complexity of relationships between Palestinian workers and owners, both living and working under occupation, and both, somewhat differently, supporting the intifada. The UNLU has consistently recognized the Palestinian factory owners as playing a key role in the uprising. *Nida'* #13 called on factory owners to "increase their production, to hire more workers, and not to deduct from workers' wages on general strike days, nor dismiss them or decrease their wages." The goal was two-fold: to increase the availability of Palestinian goods to encourage a broader boycott of Israeli products; and to provide financial support for Palestinians faced with being fired because of the intifada or who quit their jobs to avoid working for Israeli companies.

The UNLU called on owners to reorganize the work week, and not to dock workers' wages for days missed because of strikes. Most agreed with the ideas, but some still insisted that workers must make up strike losses through working overtime or nights.

In a small clothing factory outside Ramallah, a union organizer was discussing with the women workers why they needed a union even though that parti-cular factory owner, a Palestinian, supports the intifada. "We have to think about the consequences of the intifada," she said. "If you live in Kalandia or Jabaliya refugee camps, and they get put under curfew, maybe your employer won't pay when you don't come in to work. So what do you ask of the employer? This employer, at this factory, didn't deduct wages even for women who couldn't come during the 40-day siege of Jalazon camp — but what about other owners?"

The head of one of the three General Federations of Trade Unions in the West Bank described some of the problems facing workers in Palestinian-owned plants. "They're now overloaded with demands for increased production. But there is no increased wage. No annual wages that include a paid vacation. The owners claim to support strike days, but still make the workers work 48-hour weeks, making up time lost with overtime. Before the intifada, some owners wanted an alliance with Jordan to make more money. Now, with the boycott of Israeli goods, they have expanded markets here in the West Bank, so they support national demands. Now they support building local markets and local alternatives to Israeli products."

An official of a different federation added that "all organizations here now are nationalist. There is a struggle just to survive; even some owners support the unions. Mostly the owners forget trying to get higher profits during the intifada. When they decide not to buy from Israel, everyone in the West Bank will get used to there being only one kind of bread."

More serious problems face those Palestinians who work inside the Green Line, in Israeli-owned factories. In Call #11, the UNLU "lauds the heroic workers who were in the forefront, participating massively in the strikes, abstaining from work in Israeli projects and permanently stopping work in the settlements.

We call upon local work places to employ as many of these workers as possible." Many workers have been fired by Israeli employers during the uprising, sometimes for missing work on strike days, other times for no reason at all. Those dismissals of Palestinians have been treated as a "voluntary quit" by Israeli Labor Court hearings, insuring that no unemployment benefits would apply.

The chance of unemployment insurance protecting a Palestinian worker inside Israel is highly unlikely. According to Rosenbluth, Israeli labor codes are available only in English and Hebrew; no Arabic translations can be found. Palestinian workers inside Israel play a critical role in the beleaguered Israeli economy, precisely because the semi-clandestine army of workers providing low-paid day labor gets virtually none of the benefits and protections due Israeli workers in the same jobs.

Israel's National Insurance Institute does in fact deduct money from Palestinians working inside the Green Line. But of the 13 assorted insurance benefits those deductions provide for Israeli Jews, Palestinian workers by law receive only three. The 13 include unemployment insurance, widows' pension, retraining after job-related injury, workers' compensation for injury, insurance against employer bankruptcy, and a wide variety of health-related benefits. The only ones legally available for Palestinians are employer bankruptcy (whose additional premiums are paid entirely by the employer rather than by the state); workers' compensation (for those few Palestinians with access to a lawyer); and maternity benefits (but only if the baby is born in an Israeli hospital. Palestinians, including women in labor, are forbidden by military order to spend the night inside the Green Line without special permission from the military authorities. So giving birth in Israeli hospitals is quite rare. Israeli Jewish women are covered for full mater-

nity benefits no matter where in the world they give birth.)

Access to workplace benefits used to be determined solely by place of residence, with full benefits available only for those living inside Israel. Palestinians from Gaza or the West Bank were administratively removed from the rolls. When Jewish settlers in the West Bank complained of being similarly removed, a slight modification was made to accommodate their growing numbers. In 1978 the restrictions were amended to say that anyone who would be eligible for Israeli citizenship under the Law of Return (which allows any Jew from anywhere in the world to claim immediate citizenship in Israel, with all attendant benefits), would also have a right to the same insurance package available to an Israeli Jew living inside the Green Line.

Palestinian workers inside the Green Line have essentially no protection. Because their work — indeed, their very presence inside the Green Line — is controlled by special Military Labor Orders, they cannot join the Histadrut, the powerful, Labor Party-linked federation of Israeli trade unions. A trade union leader in Gaza noted "there can be no relations between our union and the Histadrut; how could we have a relationship with them while Israeli workers, in their role as soldiers during their twice-a-year reserve stints, come and kill us here in Gaza?" He noted that the president of the Histadrut, Israel Ketzhar, a Labor Party leader, fully supports Defense Minister Rabin's intifada policies. "He [Ketzhar] visited Ansar III prison camp in the Negev desert, and someone asked him if he would help the arrested trade unionists there. He answered 'these people are not like our unionists, they are political.' We do have good relations with some people in the Democratic Front for Peace and Equality [the Arab-based Israeli electoral front led by the Israeli Communist Party] and with grassroots members of the Histadrut. Some of them have even supported our call for an independent state. . . . But the Histadrut itself didn't even respond to any of the acts of anti-worker repression during the uprising, even the incident in the first months of the uprising where three workers were burned to death." In that instance, Palestinian workers had been locked inside a building overnight inside the Green Line, by a factory owner concerned about the laws forbidding Palestinians to remain overnight inside Israel.

Inside Israel, Palestinian unions from the West Bank and Gaza have no legal status at all.

During the uprising, the numbers of Palestinians working inside the Green Line has been sharply reduced. In the West Bank, by the end of the first year, only 35,000 to 40,000 of an estimated 110,000 Palestinians were still working inside the Green Line. Of Gaza's much smaller total population, the same number of workers used to work inside Israel. During the intifada, only about 30,000 of 100,000 workers continue to travel daily to work across the Green Line.

The impact of up to 135,000 newly unemployed Palestinians is a serious one. The Israeli Ministry of Labor, trying to put extra pressure on low-paid Palestinian workers, announced that unemployment among Israelis is up too. Other officials threatened to bring Portuguese, Greek, or other European "guest workers" to Israel to replace Palestinians in the lowest paid job categories. In March 1988, the military governor told one of the union federation heads that he intended to bring in European workers. "Go ahead and try it, I told him," the union offical recalled. "But it won't work — the wages aren't high enough. Besides, no one will accept to work under the same conditions as Palestinian workers, paying the same taxes as Israelis but getting no health or social insurance, no protection against firing, nothing."

Palestinian trade unions have a long history. Before 1967, there was one trade union federation, linked to the Jordanian unions. When the Israeli occupation began, the trade unions were shut down for two years. The federation was allowed to reopen, briefly, in 1969. Shortly after, the newly elected independent head of the federation was deported.

After 1970, the unions cut relations with Jordan, and formed the independent General Federation of Trade Unions in the occupied territories. Although there are now three separate federations, all share a similar involvement in Palestinian national life. As Israel's own economy became more and more dependent on the cheap labor of the Palestinian "black market," the role of the Palestinian unions in the occupied territories increased as well.

The role of Palestinian workers as a group has long been a decisive one in the occupied territories. Since 1967, when the occupation itself transformed a largely rural, agricultural population into a far more urbanized, worker-oriented society, Palestinian workers and their organizations have played central roles in the nationalist efforts.

At the beginning of the intifada, it was the unions' crucial decision to call for a general strike, a strike that lasted over a month, that made possible the consolidation of the intifada as a society-wide phenomenon.

Later in the intifada, that importance was reflected in the harsh repression directed at the unions. The role of the 85 unions grouped in the three federations in helping to create an independent Palestinian economy, made them natural targets for an occupation authority intent on suppressing any expression of nationalism. One federation, at the end of the uprising's first year, had three executive committee members and 31 of its 38 council members in prison. Another had seven of 13 members of its executive committee in prison, and two offices shut down. Twenty-eight heads of trade union committees have been arrested during the intifada, and donations from outside were severely limited.

"Attacks on unions are not new to the intifada," Rosenbluth said. "There have been continuous attacks for years, but the scale now is much higher. In the past, four or five unions would face one- to six-month closures; now 30 unions were closed for two years each. In past years, a total of about 10 unionists were held in administrative detention. Administrative detainees are imprisoned on the order of an Israeli military commander. They are not charged with any crime, and have no rights to judicial review. Now there are 30 to 40, just counting known trade union leaders, in addition to hundreds of rank-and-file unionists, with no accurate list of all of them. Adnan Dagher, from the General Workers Union in Ramallah, was among those expelled in August of 1988."

The political role of Palestinian unions is not new to the uprising. The Jerusalem Electrical Company's union has played a key role in the struggle to keep the company Arab-based. The JEC, originally a British-owned concession during the British Mandate's control of Palestine before the creation of Israel, was divided in 1948 into an Israeli company and a Jerusalem/West Bank company. According to Abd al-Diab, an executive at JEC, "up until 1987 the [Arab] JEC had 1,200,000 customers, but Israel was still preventing us from using our new power station. . . . On January 1 of this year, Jewish consumers in Jerusalem shifted to the Israeli company — for political, not economic reasons. The JEC is 38% owned by several Arab municipalities — Ramallah, El Bireh, Bethlehem, Beit Sahour and Jericho — and 62% by individual Arab stockholders. The Jerusalem municipal section was controlled by Israel. Israel wants to merge the Jerusalem sector with the Israeli com-

pany, but the workers in our union refused. Israel gave a military order and jailed the striking workers."

"We need Palestinian factories to hire more workers," he added, "so we have fewer workers going to work inside Israel. It has a serious economic effect on Israel when Palestinian workers don't go to their jobs. It forces the army recruits to staff the factories. . . . We have high trade union consciousness among workers, but their consciousness first is as Palestinians."

A JEC worker from Dheisha camp, a union member for 23 years, described how "the company pays when we miss work as a result of curfews. This was demanded by the union. It's a good union. It fights for the rights of workers. Even if the owners support the intifada, workers still need to struggle for their rights."

The uprising has posed new challenges to the trade union federations. The first, most agree, is unity. "In the intifada, unity comes from the street," a federation official said. Then, "the trade union federation is preparing to force an agreement between factory owners and the workers' committee — to forge a new Palestinian Labor Law. This is not the time to let the factory owners do what they wish. We must move now when the ball is in our court. Our agreement calls for one month annual leave, health and social insurance, two months pregnancy leave. We have the force of the street, the force of the intifada to pressure them, but we also face high unemployment. We need to study wages, workers' lives, to justify and explain our new agreement.

"This is a new period for us. The life of the people is the life of the intifada. That won't change quickly. We must work to prepare for a long period. We work in the field to organize more workers into unions. People used to be afraid of trade unions because the authorities were against them, but with the intifada people are not afraid of anyone. We must take advantage of this courage."

The Children and Youth

The vision of the Palestinian uprising that has captured the imagination of the world is that of the "children of the stones," young Palestinians facing the might of the Israeli military machine armed with nothing but stones. It is a David and Goliath image that finally reversed a carefully constructed mythology of Israel as the beleaguered David. And indeed, the youth of the intifada's activists is very much a part of why and how the uprising emerged as it did. For these are children, teenagers and young adults who have known nothing but military occupation for their entire conscious lives. They have known nothing else, and they are not afraid.

"We have to remember that 75% of the population of the West Bank is under 28 years old, which makes us a very young society compared to the rest of the world," said a graduate student from Bir Zeit University. "And we have been under occupation for over 20 years, which means we have a new generation, a Palestinian generation, born under occupation. This generation does not know anything but Israeli military rules, Israeli military oppression, demolition of houses, settlement building and soldiers patrolling the streets beating up Palestinians. This is their image of the occupation. That is why they took the lead at the beginning of the uprising, and that is why they are right now fighting the occupation and making the uprising more successful."

In Gaza's Khan Yunis camp, a young student from the Baptist-run nursing school in Gaza City brought together a group of his friends for a discussion of the uprising with us. The young men were in their teens and early 20s, but they possessed a sophisticated grasp of the complexities of Palestinian politics.

They were also unwavering in their

recognition of the intersection between the PLO and the leadership. "The intifada has been approved by PLO members," one said. "They are the united leadership."

"The PLO is in every person," another young Palestinian said. "I am Yasir Arafat, I am George Habash, I am all of them. The important thing is our goal — that the intifada should help us win an independent state led by the PLO."

The new preeminent role of young people in Palestinian society has challenged certain assumptions about age. Akram Haniyeh, in Geneva, cited pre-intifada social and economic factors causing the changes. He described how Palestinians during the years of occupation had to seek jobs outside their village, often working for Israelis inside the Green Line, when traditional family farmland was confiscated or access to water was cut by the military authorities.

"The role of youth outside the family is changing significantly in this period," he said. "Before, people stayed mostly inside their extended family circle until they married. Now, even at 15, a Palestinian teenager is much more independent. Nuclear family ties have lessened as social ties based on ideas and people outside the family increased."

The transformation of Palestinian youth, in village, camp or town, into *shebab*, represents a new phase in this changing identity. The word *shebab*, roughly translated, means "the guys," and is used as a term of both respect and endearment. The *shebab* are the young people on the front lines of confrontation with Israeli soldiers. Their contribution to the reorganization of Palestinian social and communal life has been tremendous.

"The *shebab* are building a new culture for young people here," said a popular committee leader in Qabatiya. "They used to spend time in cafes, playing cards. We even had some drug prob-

lems here. Now none of that goes on. The leadership of the *shebab* say it is not allowed for their members to hang around in the cafes."

The older people in general recognize the leadership of the youth during the uprising. "They deal with all our problems here in the village now," said an older resident of Beita. "Even some of the problems we used to have with the young men bothering the girls going for water. Now if any of the young men wait for the girls, the *shebab* themselves deal with it." The average age of these young men is 22; they range from 17 to 30 years old.

The young women face other problems. In some areas, especially in the refugee camps and cities, young girls are part of the *shebab*, with or without their parents' knowledge. Throwing stones, building barricades, organizing protest marches — all involve the teenaged girls.

In other areas, however, especially in the villages, girls are prevented by tradition and family strictures from participating with the boys. The girls also face special problems at the hands of Israeli soldiers.

The mother of three teenaged girls in Jabaliya Camp in Gaza described how "the Israeli director of the camp gathered all of us mothers together, and told us he could not guarantee the safety of girls and women because the soldiers were in the street, and he would not protect them." She said she thinks the threats were designed to scare the women and girls to prevent them from participating in the work of the uprising.

"But I have to take the warning seriously," she went on. "Now when I go shopping, I go myself, I can't send my daughters. But I don't like to go to the market and leave my older girls alone. I'm afraid of what the soldiers might do. If I'm there I can try to protect them."

One of the most serious problems facing young Palestinians during the in-

47

tifada revolves around the closing of schools. Early in the uprising, the Israelis decided that the schools had become centers of "violent resistance" and had to be shut down. But a report on "Israel's War Against Education" issued by Al-Haq, the West Bank affiliate of the Geneva-based International Commission of Jurists, shows that the "Israeli authorities' conduct toward academic activity during the last 11 months does not indicate a concern for security. Rather, due to their breadth, the procedures used [to close the schools] appear to be designed to penalize the community as a whole. Closure orders, for example, have not been issued solely to schools where 'violent demonstrations' were alleged to have occurred. Instead, all 1,194 West Bank schools were closed simultaneously without regard for activities at any specific location."

With a generally young population, it is not surprising that students compose about 40% of the West Bank population. Al-Haq figures indicate that about 300,000 school-age children and 18,000 college and university students have been affected by the school closures. (For various short periods, a few religious and private schools, and the schools in East Jerusalem, were exempted from the closures.)

One answer to the school shutdown was the development of "popular education," initiated by Palestinians in the first months after the schools were closed. This referred to a system of alternative schooling, where unemployed teachers and community residents would teach groups of students in homes, back yards, basements, mosques and churches.

Popular education soon became a threat to the Israeli occupation — not a security threat, certainly, but a direct challenge for political control of the West Bank and Gaza. It was part of the creation of dual power, denying to the authorities the uncontested command of

day-to-day Palestinian life. As a result, popular education was outlawed. By military order, teachers face arrest for conducting small classes for their neighbors' children. According to the *Jerusalem Post* (Nov. 25, 1988), "the implication of 'popular education' . . . was not lost on the authorities and the bucolic classes under the trees were quickly curtailed. In several cases, the army entered private homes to disperse children who had gathered for informal tutoring sessions." Al-Haq reports "in October . . . the Israeli military also informed schools that actions such as passing out workbooks to primary and secondary school children for home study would not be tolerated."

The concept of popular education, nonetheless, remained a key component of the intifada. Children learned new security rules along with history and spelling. Even the six and seven-year-olds knew they must carry their books and pencils hidden in plastic bags of bread, not in schoolbags, so the soldiers would not follow them.

The clandestine classes themselves created a level of enthusiasm and excitement from the students far beyond that of a normal classroom setting. A fourth-grade Arabic grammar class convened one evening in the hidden bedroom of a house just outside the Al-Amari refugee camp. The children, nine girls and one lone boy, were all nine and 10 years old. Hands waved in the air, fingers snapping to attract the teacher's attention. "Ustaz, ustaz," they shouted, begging the teacher to call on them.

Popular education has raised the broader problem of the insufficiency of Palestinian education under occupation. The curriculum is based on the old Jordanian curriculum; the only changes made were those mandated by the Israeli authorities after 1967. Only now, with the advent of popular education, have Palestinian teachers and professors begun to take up the challenge of developing a truly Palestinian curriculum.

In the interim, what emerged in popular education was what some called "revolutionary education." All subjects are taught through discussion of the occupation and the uprising. In the fourth-grade grammar lesson, the teacher wrote a sentence on the board, and asked his pupils to find the verb. The sentence was: "The students heard about the *nida'at*" (referring to the communiques of the uprising leadership).

The system has expanded in some areas to include adult classes. A clandestine adult Hebrew class meeting one night in the Ramallah suburb of El Bireh, brought together almost a dozen students with a no-nonsense teacher whose fluent Hebrew reflected her childhood inside the Green Line. "We now have more students in the Hebrew classes," one student said. "People need to be able to understand the language of the occupier. We need to watch their television news and understand what the soldiers in the street are yelling."

But underground education is only a stop-gap measure, and the children continue to pay a high price for the school closures. "Our program of popular education is not sufficient," a Beit Sahour leader said. "It can't really fill the gap left by the schools closing. . . . Underground schools were established in the neighborhoods, but we had insufficient teachers in all the schools, even for teaching the basics — science, Arabic, English, math. Preparatory and secondary schools were even more difficult. We need specialized teachers, but they are not always available in every neighborhood. It's hard to keep the schools secret. Teachers have to travel, books may be discovered by the military and teachers are afraid of their houses being demolished. Now with popular schools outlawed, it's even forbidden to teach our own children at home. . . . There is no solution in sight for the education problem. The problem of edu-cation is a catastrophe for us. The real aim of the Israelis is not their security, but collective punishment of the Palestinians. It is an effort to keep us ignorant, uneducated — to disrupt school life."

The children face additional problems as well. The omnipresence of the uprising in daily life means that the children are exposed early to the realities of occupation and repression, and quickly begin to imitate the resistance of their parents and older brothers and sisters. But they simultaneously face new adjustments and challenges often beyond their emotional maturity.

"I have a nephew, four years old," a Bir Zeit University lecturer said. "He wants to go out into the street to play. What are they playing right now? They're playing building roadblocks. One day when he was playing with the kids in the neighborhood, my sister asked him not to play that game, saying that the soldiers would come. The children looked at her and laughed. With stones in their hands, they said, 'well, let them come.' That was their immediate answer. So this reflects that first of all, they have no fear of the soldiers, no fear of the occupation, and they are ready to confront the occupation. So how does this affect our children? Well, in a way it's positive, because they have more awareness of the situation. They move so quickly from a stage of childhood to a stage of maturity."

A member of one of the women's organizations said in Ramallah, "the kids are maturing so quickly. I have a neighbor, and he came to complain to me that they wouldn't let him be part of the neighborhood committee, because he's only seven years old. They told him he couldn't be in the committee unless he was over 13, so he said, 'but I can throw stones, I can do all that.' We had to explain to him that the neighborhood committee had to do other things too, like guarding, storing food, education. We told him he could be part of the education committee since he was in school. And he said 'okay, I can study, but in the morning I can stand guard with the others.' So now you feel that the children even understand that it's not just throwing stones, that there are other responsibilities, and they feel these responsibilities too. So it's positive, but it's negative too, somehow."

The kindergarten and nursery teachers are perhaps the first to face the psychological problems of children growing up in the intifada. One kindergarten supervisor described some of the causes of those problems. "We have a kindergarten in Bir Zeit village, for example. The army often comes into the village, and the kids face all kinds of restrictions, especially during curfews. Some are afraid of the soldiers, and cry and want to leave or hide. Others throw rocks. Their reactions reflect the different views of their families in how to respond to soldiers. But it's always difficult for them."

She described how weekly meetings for teachers and supervisors, to discuss psychological problems and potential solutions, are held on a district-wide level. "We try to encourage the kids not to be frightened of the soldiers," the teacher said. "We tell them that all Palestinians must continue their work during the intifada, and that their work is kindergarten. We find that teaching ideas of resistance, and especially the idea of cooperating with others to resist, eases some psychological problems. We also have particular problems to respond to when children are faced with having their house demolished, or their father killed or sent to prison."

Another kindergarten teacher, in Dheisha camp, spoke of "the changes in children since the intifada began. In the past, if I asked a kid to sing, they would sing about their fathers, mothers or about the land. Now, they will sing of the intifada, of stones, of the *fedayeen* (guerrillas). They learn songs in the street

from the *shebab*, and we teach them songs too. Before, their games were things like playing house; now they play soldiers and *shebab*, or play at helping the wounded to the hospital. This we don't teach, but they learn in the streets.

"Children's feelings grow against the occupation," she said. "When they play soldiers and *shebab*, the 'youth' throw stones and sometimes pretend to be injured. Nowadays, when they play building games, they build guns instead of tables. They used to draw houses or trees; now they draw soldiers.

"But of course they have psychological problems. They often talk about the soldiers, they talk about family members who have been arrested and sometimes they are afraid. As teachers, we want to give children a normal life. We want to help develop their normal childhood feelings, but that is difficult to accomplish. Our children now live complicated lives and we are unable give them a normal life.

"Our kids are victims. All over the world people know of the plight of Palestinian children. It's good for us that our kids will know how to react to soldiers, but it's sad because we can't give the kids a normal life. Jewish society gives Jewish children everything they need; that's normal in any society. Palestinian kids should get everything too, but we can't give it to them because of the occupation."

Yet the children remain the hope of the Palestinians, the hope of the intifada. Mahmoud Tayyam, the vice-president of the Palestine National Council, reflected how "[Israeli Prime Minister Yitzhak] Shamir hoped that when the generation of Palestinians of the past, who lived at the time of the occupations of 1948 and 1967, had grown old and died, that the Palestinian problem would die too. But now all those throwing stones are of the new generation and the Palestinian problem is still alive."

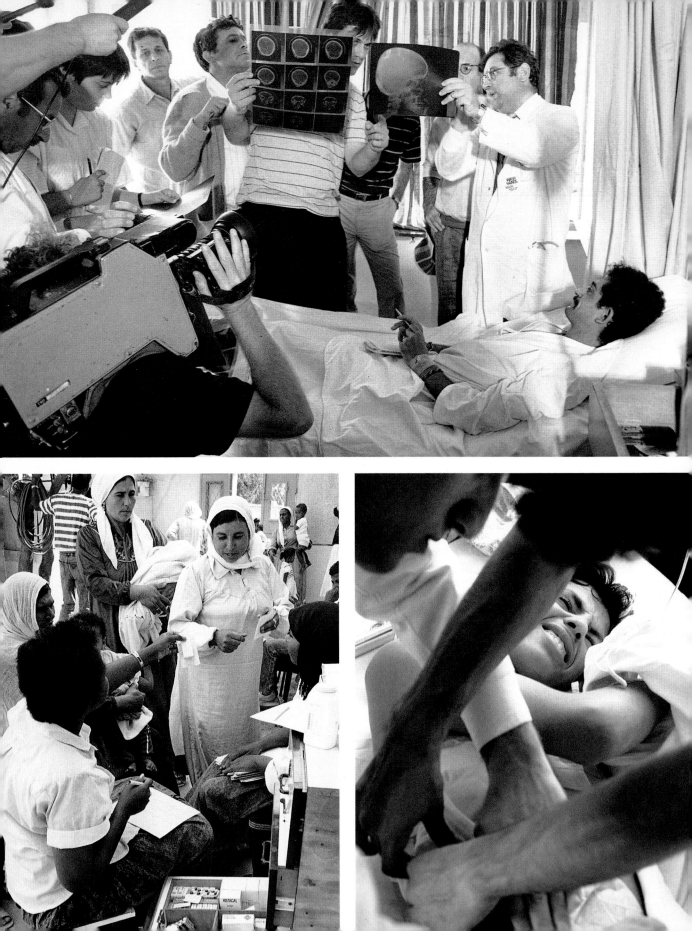

The Doctors
and Medical Workers

Israel's military tactics have been nothing if not innovative. But, at bottom, these measures are all designed to suppress the uprising, and the human toll paid by the Palestinians is horrific.

The new, and old, weapons have severely challenged the Palestinian health care systems. The massive use of toxic, often lethal American-made CS tear-gas; the development of "plastic" bullets made up largely of zinc and glass; rubber bullets whose metal core sometimes comes loose from its coating to penetrate the body; new rubber-wrapped steel spheres the size and weight of a large marble; shiny, foil-wrapped packets engineered to explode in flames when opened; as well as standard live ammunition, clubs and sticks for beating — together produce a litany of daily injuries to scores, often hundreds, of Palestinians, and a nightmarish demand on medical resources.

All of this is taking place in a situation where general health conditions were already poor, and medical professionals and institutions were already understaffed, underfunded, and often unable to function during the 20 years of occupation. Dr. Mustafa Barghouti, director of the Medical Relief Committee (MRC), one of several popular Palestinian medical groups, is firm that "the intifada, and our work within it, cannot be separated from what existed before. In the past, MRC was formed to respond to the health needs created by Israel's efforts to undermine Palestinian health services and replace them with Israeli institutions, creating dependency on Israel."

That dependency, however, insured inadequate health services. Dr. Barghouti quoted figures from the official Israeli Statistical Abstracts showing that between 1975 and 1985, the West Bank's population grew by 21%. In the same period, hospital beds were reduced by 6%. In Gaza, the population grew by 26%, hospital beds were down 13%.

Dr. Barghouti described the two main tendencies among health care professionals before the intifada. "The first group didn't confront the occupation. They tried to improve the existing conditions in Israeli government-run hospitals serving the Palestinians. But they failed because there was no space within those existing Israeli organizations to function and serve the Palestinian population. The second group worked through charitable organizations, separate from the occupation authorities. They functioned as an alternative to Israeli institutions, and were legal under Israeli law. But they had constant fights for licenses and faced the constant threat of being shut down for technical violations. They achieved some success. However, they faced serious obstacles from Israel. In Gaza for 10 years, the Red Crescent Society was denied a permit to build a new hospital.

"In general, Israeli policies were designed to keep the Palestinian population dependent on the occupation authorities for services, even if what they provide is completely insufficient.

"Now there's a new spirit," Dr. Barghouti added. "The MRC and others began to organize on a popular basis. Now, we refuse to seek permission and do not respect the context of the Israeli laws to regulate our licensing. Anyway, the strength of any health institution is in the people, not in machines or buildings that could be closed down. In some ways, Israel even helped in our development. The occupation made any other approach impossible, and forced us to create our own institutions."

In Call #3, issued little more than a month after the uprising began, the Unified Leadership appealed "to the doctors and health service personnel: We ask you to constantly be on call and immediately join the health committees which

53

organize medical aid campaigns for the camps and districts under siege. We ask all doctors, pharmacists, nurses and lab technicians to participate in the medical aid campaigns. Health conditions are deteriorating and we are suffering from rampant disease in the camps and the occupied territories generally, as a result of sieges, starvation, and the use of poisonous gases. To the owners of medical supply factories and pharmacies: We ask you to make a broad campaign of medical donations to the medical committees in order for them to give free treatment to the injured."

In response, MRC identified two deceptively simple goals: to continue its existing work, and to be able to meet new challenges. "We faced a lot of difficulties in the first few months," the director said. "We needed to dramatically expand our capacity. For example, when we began sending out mobile clinics to small villages and camps in 1982, we made only 40 trips that year. Last year, in 1987, we had 350 trips, a significant increase. This year we have already made 700 trips, treating 80,000 people."

By the time *nida'a* #14 was issued on April 20th, the UNLU raised the ante, challenging the medical providers to meet new tasks in the new period: "The work of the health committees should be expanded, to help our people everywhere. There should be courses in first-aid, preventive medicine and health awareness. We call upon our brother doctors to decrease their fees in support of the uprising."

Since that time, one of the most important areas of work for the medical organizations has been in paramedic and first-aid training. The UNLU's call reflected the reality that many camps and villages do not have doctors or nurses in residence, and that emergency conditions often do not allow medical teams to enter. This is especially true during curfew periods, when frequent clashes often

lead to multiple casualties, with no access to medical treatment because doctors are kept out of the area.

The Boston-based Physicians for Human Rights reports that "Israeli soldiers repeatedly barred ambulances, doctors and health teams from their work in refugee camps and villages when there were no demonstrations, particularly in communities that had been placed under curfew. . . . At every hospital, clinic, physician's office and UNRWA [United Nations Relief and Works Agency] facility our team visited, we were told with special urgency of repeated instances in which Israeli soldiers and police had refused entry to ambulances, physicians and other health workers trying to reach the victims of beatings and shootings. These reports were precise and specific . . ."

These Israeli efforts have not kept medical teams out altogether. Each of the medical organizations has stories of their successful entry to areas under curfew. With the *shebab* standing guard, doctors and nurses are smuggled, often by women, into the camp or village through secret passages unknown to the occupying soldiers.

But entering closed areas is a risky and uncertain proposition. To create a better chance of at least basic immediate care, the medical groups, in conjunction with the popular committees and the women's associations, mobilized a massive first-aid training campaign which aimed at making skilled emergency and trauma care accessible to every Palestinian.

During the first year of the intifada, over 35,000 people, mostly young women, were trained in emergency care. This is not the perfunctory bandaging practice of Boy Scout summer camp, but rather a rigorous course of up to 20 separate sessions. They were instructed on how to deal with fractures, gas inhalation, cardiac arrest and other serious, but all-too-common intifada emergencies. Tens of thousands of comprehensive first-aid kits have been distributed and stored in schools, mosques or homes until needed.

During one first-aid class, in the small village of El-Khader, near Bethlehem, the doctor began by checking attendance. "We want to be sure that all our students are actually capable of giving emergency care," he said. Students who miss a class are contacted later, and are given separate make-up instruction.

This class was run by the Union of Health Care Committees in the occupied territories which was founded in 1985. The 21 young women in the course ranged in age from 13 to 30 years. The doctor began with a review of last week's lecture, dealing with cardiac massage and artificial respiration. Today's lesson was on reading vital signs and on the use of thermometers and blood pressure cuffs, how to take a pulse, and how to evaluate the readings.

The class was enthusiastic and attentive, although occasional distractions showed how even the urgency of learning emergency medical skills has become part of the routine of Palestinian life during the intifada. One group of girls clustered around, admiring a student's new gold watch. Later in the class, the announcement that someone's sister had gotten engaged caused a brief flurry of excitement. And the small baby of the house where the class was held was fussed over and passed from one student to another.

But no one missed the seriousness of purpose in this class. These girls had seen all too often the need for skills such as those they were learning. I asked the doctor if he minded Neal photographing him, since teaching such a class could easily result in arrest and perhaps administrative detention. He responded, "why not? If Israel asks me, I will say this is not a political meeting, it's just a first-aid class."

"They can kill us," the doctor added. "What can they do more than that? More than killing all of us they can't do anything. What can they do to me? I am only one of a million Palestinians here on the West Bank. . . . Everybody here is treated the same by the soldiers. It doesn't matter if you're a doctor, an engineer or a scientist. If you are against colonialism or Zionism, you're treated the same."

The doctors' work is not limited to intifada cases. General health conditions, already poor, have seriously deteriorated during the intifada, as Israel cut back its already skimpy provision of health services in the occupied territories. A major blow came in the middle of the first year of the uprising. Israel announced what the Los Angeles Times called "a decision by military authorities in the occupied West Bank to sharply curtail hospital care for needy Arabs living under Israeli rule. In some cases, up to 80% of hospitalization days were cut back by the authorities for the treatment of grave diseases that hospitals in the occupied area are unequipped to handle. The West Bank's military-dominated Civil Administration argued that Palestinians, by reducing tax payments during the Arab uprising, are due fewer services." Even though many Palestinian physicians (and a number of Israeli doctors as well) refused to abide by the new restrictions, the fear of being turned away kept many people from seeking treatment at hospitals.

The popular medical organizations have helped to patch some of the gaps in the health care system. At 9:00 a.m. one morning, the office/clinic on the edge of East Jerusalem is a beehive of activity. The women from the village medical workers' class are about to start a lecture on intestinal disorders; the first patients are arriving for well-baby check-ups; and the mobile clinic teams are checking their vans.

The medical van, loaded with equipment to set up an instant primary-care clinic, headed out for a small village in the Jordan valley. Picking up four local nurses at villages on the way, the team arrived at Al-Nusseriah, population about 300, and set up the clinic in the rooms and courtyard of the largest house in the village. The mosque loudspeaker called the people, announcing the clinic was opening for free medical care. The team was composed of two doctors, a dentist, one lab technician, and the four nurses.

Patients ranged from an old woman with neuralgia, high blood pressure and arteriosclerosis (given hypertension medication and told to reduce salt in her diet), to a small baby with severe diaper rash (his mother given a local ointment and instructions to let him crawl around naked). Several pregnant women were examined, most of them insisting that the doctors (both male) probe their abdomen only through several layers of clothes. "Being unable to examine the women is a serious problem," a doctor said. "Often I have to base a diagnosis more on what a patient says she feels, than on what I could tell with a full exam."

Throughout the day, 30 patients were examined. A total of 40 villagers, including patients as well as their friends and neighbors, had their blood analyzed. The blood-typing campaign is one of the clearest examples of how Palestinian institutions have responded to the new demands posed by the intifada.

"The blood-typing project was initiated by the lab technicians themselves," Dr. Barghouti explained. "On February 8, 1988, 30 people were brought to Al-Makassad hospital with gunshot wounds from Israeli soldiers. The hospital ran out of blood early. There was a public call made. Hundreds of people re-sponded, but it took hours to process and type all the blood. So the idea started for registering blood donors all over the West Bank. We now have 24,000 people and their blood types listed at neighborhood, regional and central levels, although we still have a problem getting the names onto a computer. Now we can meet virtually any blood need in the West Bank or Gaza. In May, 15 gunshot victims were brought to Ramallah Hospital on the same day. They called, and within one hour we got 22 donors there with the right blood types.

"One of our goals is to train village health workers," one of the mobile clinic doctors said. The committee runs a nine-month course designed to prepare people to handle basic health education and training, as well as broader public health needs. Public health and hygiene conditions in the more remote villages are rudimentary at best. Many camps and villages have streams of raw sewage running down unpaved streets where the children play. Others have had their electricity cut for months as collective punishment during the uprising, preventing, in some cases, clean water supplies from being pumped. The medical teams spend much of their time treating patients with skin and urinary tract infections. These and other conditions are caused by the unsanitary plumbing and sewage facilities, or by the lack of pure water.

"We need good relations with the community. The local village health committees include both traditional leaders and young people. The traditional leaders think they're in charge, but it is the young people that really do the work," one of the doctors said. The committees distribute pamphlets and information on birth control, care of fractures and other topics such as first-aid, infant care, nutrition and hygiene.

"It's especially important to train women," the mobile clinic doctor said

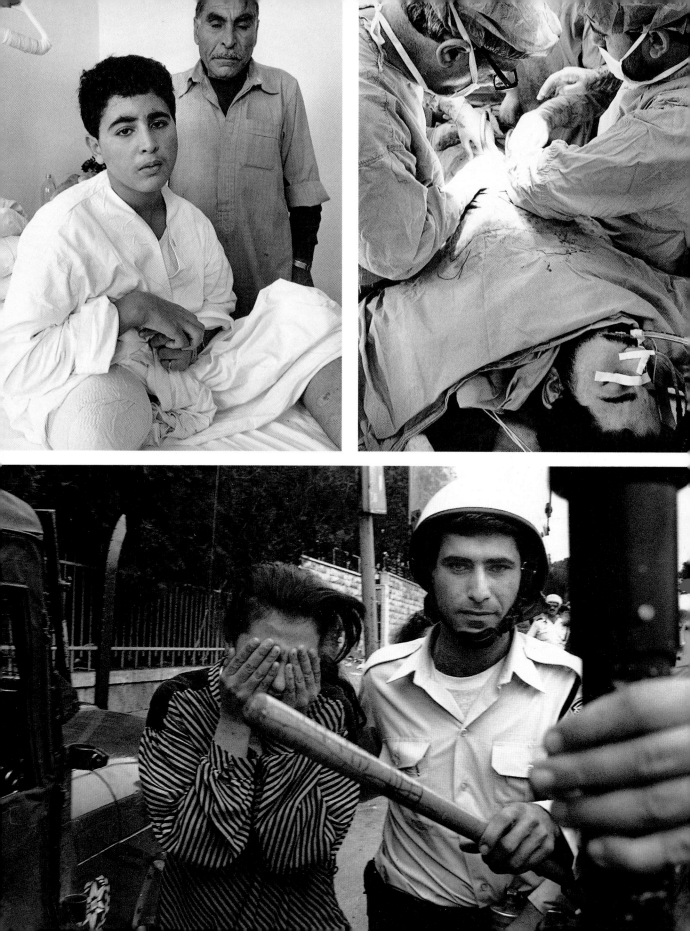

during a break in the stream of patients, "since women make up 90% of those needing primary health care in these villages, and women can deal with the community much better. Women doctors can treat men in the villages, but not vice-versa. The democratic nature of groups like MRC provides an outlet for women doctors facing discrimination. In the West Bank as a whole, only 8% of the doctors are women; in MRC, 32% are women."

Al-Makassad Hospital, in Jerusalem, remains the flagship of the Palestinian health care system. Al-Makassad's director, Dr. Rustom Nammary, described the challenges his hospital faces daily. "We get all the injuries from the Jerusalem area, Hebron, and all the camps in those areas," he said. "We also get referrals for major injuries from all over the West Bank. . . . Al-Makassad is the only place for neurosurgery and cardiac surgery. One patient was brought in at 1 a.m. yesterday from Gaza, and another from Nablus. For many patients, hemodialysis is only available here. The equipment is available in Ramallah, Hebron and Nablus, but only in government hospitals. So patients have to pay because of the military order forbidding free treatment."

"We get all kinds of injuries here," Dr. Nammary added. "Some of the beatings are so severe, I have never seen anything like it in my life." He described beatings causing epidural hematoma, or bleeding inside the skull. "We have treated over 4,000 injuries here, on an out-patient basis during the intifada. Another 400 were admitted to the hospital. So far we have the ability to cope with the overload because we have all the specialities here. On several occasions we have had to send patients to other hospitals in the middle of the night to make room for new arrivals from clashes that day."

Hospital workers are not immune from the general problems facing Palestinians during the uprising. An official of Gaza City's Al-Ahli Hospital described the most recent curfew in the fall of 1988. "We had to get special permission for our staff to come to work," he said. "In the past, the military has refused to honor the permission they said they would give. We have to be prepared now for longer sieges that affect the hospital too. We have to stock food and organize new ways of living so the staff can stay inside the hospital during the curfews and sieges. They can't drive home to Rafah or Khan Yunis at night any more. We've gotten used to the 'normal' 9 p.m. to 3 a.m. curfew in Gaza."

"We have an agreement with the civil administration," he added. "The soldiers are not allowed to enter the hospital without the permission of the hospital director. In return the hospital had to agree to provide the name and address of victims of the intifada. So it's like a very difficult give-and-take relationship.

"We also face a serious shortage of medical staff. A high number of doctors and other medical personnel have been arrested, all over the West Bank and Gaza. For example, we only have two anesthesia technicians and right now one of them is in prison for six months administrative detention. One person alone just can't stay awake long enough for all the cases."

The Palestinian health care system as a whole is gradually being absorbed into the broader network of popular organizations that characterize the resistance of the intifada. Dr. Barghouti said that "earlier in the uprising, before the popular committees were banned, we worked through them. After they were made illegal, the forms of organization changed, but it's not so different now. They are all grassroots organizations anyway. We are working in over 200 villages and camps, through youth clubs, women's organizations and pre-existing clinics. The framework of [legal] popular committees may be gone, but the people didn't change."

THE FARMERS

For generations, the Palestinians have largely been an agricultural people. Although the occupation has transformed many small farmers into underpaid laborers in Israeli factories and construction crews, traditional farming remains a way of life for hundreds of thousands of Palestinians.

But Israel's response to the intifada has threatened even the land of Palestine. Villages are often forbidden to harvest their crops. Collectively-owned olive presses are being shut down by the occupation authorities. Land is being confiscated for arbitrarily imposed security needs or stolen outright by settlers, and water sources are blocked or diverted to the swimming pools and lush technocrops of near-by settlements.

One autumn afternoon, in the tiny village of Hawwara, off the Nablus Road, Neal and I found two she-goats, two kids and five chickens, that had been shot by Israeli settlers only moments earlier. The youngest child in the family that owned these animals, about six years old, had thrown a small stone at the settlers' car as it passed the family's house. In response, the carload of six settlers entered the back of the house and fired 20 to 30 shots at the sheep and goats.

"Next time I'll come back to kill you *and* the sheep," one of the settlers shouted. Two carloads of soldiers arrived during the settler attack, and waited outside until the settlers left.

The father of the family, carrying the bodies of the dead goats outside, said "if there was a horse or a cow there, it would have been killed too. To work in Israel is bad, so we thought we would raise animals instead, but now the settlers come and kill them. It's like prison here, like jail. People don't go out at night. It's like a civilian war."

The soldiers returned while we were photographing the dead animals. As soon as they were spotted by the family, we were led into a less visible room in the house until the soldiers left some time later. We were then led across the fields to avoid the Israeli patrol.

On a broader scale, Palestinian agriculture in general has been one of the targets of Israel's efforts to suppress the intifada. According to the Jerusalem-based DataBase Project on Palestinian Human Rights, "olives and olive oil constitute the most important single crop in the West Bank. Olives are a biannual crop and peak-year production, such as that of 1988, is usually at least double that of non-peak years. . . . The olive harvest season opened on October 15. By October 24 . . . at least 12 villages had been formally prohibited from harvesting. They included Asira Ash-Shamaliya, Kufr Malek, Maythaloun, Saris, Bela', Nuba, Kharess, Burk'a, Kufr Thilith, Barta'a and Luban Ash-Sharqiya. . . . Two dunams of olive trees were burned in Al-Mazra'a Ash-Sharqiya on September 30. Olive trees were uprooted in Hawwara and El-Bireh on October 1 and again in Hawwara the next day. In Ithna, which has been under siege since the beginning of September, farmers have been prohibited from bringing their harvested olives into the village. . . ." The report goes on, with further documentation of the destruction of olive trees, the closure of oil presses, and the rotting of grape harvests on the vine.

While traditional Palestinian farming remains under attack by the occupation, new forms of food production and processing are developing. On February 19, 1988, in *nida'a #8*, the UNLU called on Palestinians to "return to our land and

till it, because it is a blessed resource for all. Many essentials can be provided from a piece of land in front of the house. Frugality will make your income last longer; it supports your steadfastness and lightens the weight of life under occupation. Vegetable gardening and keeping livestock can easily be done. Let us remember that the Vietnamese conquered U.S. tyranny not only by guns, but also by making such simple farms."

In response, in the first spring of the uprising, collective gardens bloomed throughout Palestine as a vital symbol of the resistance. Even in the towns and cities, people were clearing stones and planting in every available space. Part of the significance of the collective garden phenomenon was symbolic. No one in the wealthy market town of Ramallah was going to survive solely on home-grown tomatoes.

But clearing fields, sowing crops, and eating locally-grown produce did help to unify the otherwise disparate sectors of Palestinian society, and it did help to "lighten the weight of the occupation." When a wealthy farmer in Beit Sahour was preparing to harvest his olives, he didn't hire his usual crew of day laborers. Instead, his extended family came, with many friends from the village, to pick the fruit. And when the harvest was in, the olives and oil were shared with those who had picked, with larger portions going to those poorer families who had more immediate needs.

In *nida'a* #4, issued on January 24, 1988, in the second month of the uprising, the Unified Leadership first called for "concentrating all energy on cultivating the land, achieving maximum self-sufficiency aimed at boycotting the enemy's goods." In following communiques, the UNLU often designated one or more days to focus on building popular gardens, or on planting the soil. By *nida'a* #14, issued in April, the UNLU could "highly appreciate the response of our

people, the agricultural and popular committees, and the neighborhood committees to the land call for home gardening and cultivating the earth through agricultural cooperatives. We call upon our people and committees to expand cultivation and cooperatives to include all our beloved homeland."

One activist in Beit Sahour described how "our popular garden started in response to the UNLU's call in February or March, asking us to grow food. We started growing eggplants and tomatoes. We had people from 10 different families, and usually people would work two days a week in the garden. We cleared stones from the land and we installed irrigation pipes. Each family gave money for seeds. When we harvested, we sold the produce cheap to our neighbors and the community."

In the tiny hamlet of Jibya, near Bir Zeit village, a visiting activist from the Agricultural Relief Committee who had studied agriculture in the U.S., explained his work. Since 1983, he had been doing university extension work in Palestinian communities, including training local farmers in new techniques. He expanded his work to include soil analysis, problems caused by pesticides and insecticides, water resources, and particular problems relating to the Jordan Valley.

"Now our focus is on building home economy," he said. "We began a study one year before the intifada started and we found that 80% of the home economy work was being carried out by women. The villages started with a high degree of self-sufficiency already. They were 80 to 85% self-sufficient and they produced almost all food except things like tea, sugar and coffee. We found that more isolated villages had higher levels of self-sufficiency which enhanced the possibility of survival during long curfews."

"Since 1967, Israel tried to destroy the agriculture-based economic infrastructure of the West Bank. It flooded the

their olives this year.

"But the Israelis can't destroy everything — farmers exist, co-ops exist. They can do nothing unless they destroy the land itself. This is the third year I have farmed this land with the Agricultural Committee, but this village has been here since Roman times. My family has been here for 200 years, and even back then they came just from a neighboring village. I am optimistic about the intifada. Work here is difficult. I work for 12 hours a day. But I enjoy it. I work more and more now because it is also our main source of food. We don't know about the future, whether there will be curfews, or other problems. My farm is a source of food for the intifada."

market with cheaper Israeli goods, and actually had some success. We found that some villages in the central areas were not very self-sufficient, because they were more dependent on the Israeli goods.

"Even before the intifada, we developed a 10-year plan to build up the home economy based on organizing farmers. During the uprising, popular committees and other new forms took over that work. Agricultural Relief encouraged them and we then shifted our own focus more to providing advanced training and resources.

"In March 1988, in the fourth month of the uprising, we held a conference with most of the organizations doing agriculture-related work: the women's groups, charitable associations, the Mennonite and Swedish aid groups, and others. We gave them the results of our study, and tried to encourage coordination of work so we wouldn't duplicate scarce resources. About 60% of those groups now work together."

An activist in Kufr Nameh's Popular Agricultural Committee described the difference in approach of the two groups: "Agricultural Relief is made up of academics and other experts providing training courses and specialized materials and techniques. Our work focuses more on organizing the farmers themselves, looking toward the creation of small-scale cooperative efforts and political empowerment. Both aspects are important, so there's room for both organizations."

All the organizations recognized the key role of women in Palestinian agriculture. The Women's Agricultural Committee was formed in January 1988, during the first month of the uprising.

"Our work is based on household economy projects," a representative of the committee said. "Our survey found that women do most of the work in the villages, because men are often out working in Israeli factories. We developed a plan to go to villages and to provide services for women who work the land. We would go to villages and give lectures regarding ideas for household economy. Sometimes we would form a Women's Agricultural Committee in the village. Other times we work through existing organizations.

"The intifada made us start working to organize our committee," she went on, "especially the call in the early *nida'at* for household economy and local self-sufficiency. We talked about how some villages, like Idna, could survive a 22-day siege, because of its high level of self-sufficiency, while in some other villages people needed outside help after only two days because they were not self-sufficient enough."

In Beitello, a farming village in the hills, a local farmer was working in his cucumber fields one afternoon. The village is home to both a farmers' cooperative and a women's processing cooperative that produces pickled vegetables.

"The women's production co-op started first," he explained. "Then they needed special kinds of cucumbers and eggplants. They had to look outside our village farms to find what they needed, because we produced what would sell best in outside markets, without paying attention to local consumption or co-op needs. Now we coordinate our work between the farmers' committee and the women's co-op, especially since the intifada began. We've shifted to the kinds of vegetables they need, and they can buy everything we grow. We've now increased our overall production through using greenhouses more.

"I haven't been threatened by the Israelis about not being allowed to harvest my crops. I think it's because my village is too far away from them. But I know of attacks every day on farming. In the Jordan Valley, thousands of tons of plants and vegetables were lost because of curfews. In Burk'a, between Jenin and Nablus, people weren't allowed to pick

3.◆The Places

A visitor to the occupied West Bank has no need to ask which are the Palestinian villages and which are Israeli settlements. The land itself shows the difference.

Most of the Palestinian villages are ancient and they are made of stones dug from their own hills. They are rooted to the earth, and from a distance, their patina of age sometimes renders them indistinguishable from the land itself.

The Israeli settlements, by contrast, are new, modern. Virtually all of them began as military outposts. Their transformation into large industrial towns, or centers of religious-ideological extremism, or bedroom communities offering cheap housing for Israel's population, reflect that earlier history. The pre-fab, blockhouse-style settlements command the heights. Visibly foreign, they perch on top of the hills looking down on age-old Palestinian houses and olive groves.

Every place in Palestine has developed its own role, its own definition of the uprising. Each town, each village, each refugee camp, almost takes on a personality, shaped by the particularities of occupation in that town, village or camp, and by the political views and personalities of those who lead the resistance.

Gaza

The Gaza Strip, a narrow ribbon of desert land squeezed between Israel and Egypt, is home to the poorest of Palestine. The 650,000 Palestinians of Gaza live in towns and camps whose population density is among the highest in the world. More than three-quarters of them came to Gaza as refugees, driven from their centuries-old homes inside what is now Israel when the state was created in 1948.

The 2,500 Israeli settlers in the Strip, living mostly in Gush K'tief, a seaside resort-kibbutz, rarely come in contact with the Palestinians. A new road takes the settlers from their condominiums on the beach to their jobs in Jerusalem or Ashkelon, avoiding the dusty Arab villages and, the tense, squalid refugee camps.

During the years of Egyptian control, even before the Israeli occupation began in 1967, popular organizations were created in Gaza. Driven by the worsening economic, social and political conditions, Gazans built women's associations, trade unions, social welfare committees, and political organizations linked to the various constituent groups within the PLO.

Under Israeli rule, the intensifying repression drove many of these organizations underground. Israel's former Minister of Defense, General Ariel Sharon, based much of his political career on his brutal suppression of a 1976 resistance campaign in Gaza. Nevertheless, the popular institutions did not disappear.

So it was not surprising that the uprising began here, in the arid sands of the inhospitable Gaza Strip.

Three of the four Palestinians killed on December 8, 1987, whose deaths are said to have sparked the uprising, lived in Jabaliya. The 50,000 residents of the fetid slum make it the largest refugee camp in Gaza.

A member of Jabaliya's Popular Committee described those early days of the intifada. "We buried the four inside the camp on the same night they were killed. There was a funeral march, and slogans were chanted. Then the soldiers attacked, and there were a number of

injuries." Four thousand people challenged the soldiers in the streets of Jabaliya that night.

"The next day," the local leader went on, "there was another big demonstration in the camp. The soldiers attacked, and we had our first martyr, Hatem al-Sis. Hatem was only 17. The soldiers responded with a curfew — our first during the uprising — which lasted for 15 days.

"It was during the curfew that the demonstrations started to spread, and the uprising really began. The day after Hatem was killed there were demonstrations in Balata Camp [near Nablus in the northern West Bank]. Protests had already started near Al-Shifa Hospital [in Gaza City]. Then it soon spread to Rafah [the southern tip of Gaza], to Khan Yunis camp and then it became the intifada."

Less than a week later, on December 13, the activists of Jabaliya called another march. This time, 10,000 people violated the curfew and poured into the crowded, muddy streets of the camp. Following that march, the 13 popular committees of Jabaliya were created, based on the 13 blocks of tin-roofed cinderblock huts that make up the camp.

"At first, the work of the popular committees was to provide food for our people in Jabaliya during the curfew. Food was sent from Palestinians in nearby villages, from Gaza City, and some even from inside the Green Line [Israel's 1967 border]. The day after the first curfew began, the Democratic Front for Peace and Equality [the largely Arab Israeli electoral bloc led by Rakah, the Communist Party] sent seven truckloads of food and some warm clothes for us.

"The popular committees distributed the food and we wrote slogans on the walls explaining why the curfew was happening. At that time, popular committees were not yet forbidden, but still we wore masks over our faces. Most of our activists were already known then, and we knew we needed to be prepared to work secretly in the future.

"Then the resistance committees were formed, separately from the popular committees. They were made up of the youth, mostly between 16 and 25, and were also based in each housing block of the camp. Their leaders were local activists and representatives of the four main PLO groups. The four women's committees also began to coordinate their work more closely.

"The popular committees, and all the popular organizations, worked hard. People already had a tradition of sharing, but the work of the committees made it possible for everyone to participate fully in the intifada, without necessarily belonging to a political organization themselves. The popular organizations made the uprising into something of all the people."

"We all had different tasks. The resistance committees would organize the stone-throwing. The merchants committees on their own began to call commercial strikes. When the numbered Calls of the Unified National Leadership of the Uprising (UNLU) began to be issued, the popular committees would explain the leaflets and figure out how to implement them here. We would work to ensure that the strike days were observed, and especially that workers did not cross the Green Line on strike days."

A large part of Gaza's population works as day laborers inside the Green Line. This part of the black market in low-paid "Arab work" made the occupation very valuable to Israel's beleaguered economy. A key component of the uprising's strategy was to decrease the number of Palestinians crossing the Green Line to work, while trying to increase the nationalist, Palestinian, alternatives to dependency on Israeli jobs and Israeli consumer goods.

"By February, we had formed the Gaza branch of the UNLU. It was made up of representatives of the popular committees, the merchants, and the resistance committees. At the beginning of the uprising, it took a lot of effort by the popular committees to keep people from going to work inside Israel. After about May, the workers started abiding by the strike days on their own, so our work was much easier.

"Now everything is established, and everyone knows what to do in the uprising. Workers won't go into Israel on strike days; the youth know when to throw stones. Earlier, it took many copies of the UNLU's leaflets to make sure that everyone got the information. Now, it is enough for people to hear the new leaflet read on radio, and to write down which are the next strike days. The intifada has become normal life."

Throughout the uprising, Gaza continued to face some of the harshest Israeli repression. Houses inside the camps — the flimsy shacks that pass as houses when the occupation authorities routinely refuse to allow improvements — are demolished as collective punishment for stone-throwing.

One house, the third demolished on December 1st, had been reluctantly destroyed on soldiers' orders by the residents themselves and their neighbors. The Israeli army's use of dynamite in blowing up other houses had led to massive damage to adjoining homes, so the neighborhood had agreed to tear down the last house facing demolition that day, by their own hands.

"We built this house ourselves," the father of the family said. "It took three of us, myself, my brother and a friend, 40 days to build it. It took only 30 minutes to destroy it.

"But I don't care about the demolition of my home, or even about my son being in prison," the father went on. "We want peace and an independent state. The intifada will continue until we achieve our aim. I was very pleased with

the Declaration of Independence and I wish we could make a real state on our own land. We want our land. We depend on the intifada until we obtain our rights. We want peace, not war. The intifada is the road to peace and an independent state."

QABATIYA

The name Qabatiya resonates through the consciousness of Palestinians, a talisman of resistance to Israeli injustices, and an example of collective mobilization. The small village, isolated in the hills of the northern West Bank, seems an unlikely symbol of discipline and unity. But it played a crucial role in subverting the widespread network of collaborators that allowed the Israeli occupation authorities to maintain control during the years before the uprising.

A member of Qabatiya's popular committee described the process of resistance. "After throwing stones, the construction of the new Palestinian society begins. Through the cooperation between people, in organizing work, the construction of our society is parallel to the destruction of the Israeli occupation authorities. We will resist occupation by any means — but there is an end: the destruction of the occupation, followed by the construction of a new Palestinian society.

"Organizing in the village was partly accidental, even in February when a collaborator was killed. The Shin Bet [Israeli secret police] had come to Qabatiya. Disguised as journalists, they took photos of demonstrators from the first weeks of the uprising. A collaborator in the village had helped the Shin Bet identify people in the photographs. As a result, many of those people were later arrested and spent a long time in prison. During a demonstration that went past the collaborator's house, some stones were thrown at his house by some of the youth. This made his wife angry, and she

70

yelled 'we want to destroy you.' Soon after, the collaborator took his gun and fired right into the crowd, killing a four-year-old child and wounding 18 others.

"People had already suffered a lot from this man, and they wanted revenge. So when the child was killed emotions were sharp — they were not moderate emotions. The whole village attacked the collaborator and killed him."

Word of the collaborator's death spread quickly. For the Palestinians, it portended the end of the pro-Israeli fifth column that had for so many years undermined local resistance to the occupation. Predictably, the army leadership was furious. They too recognized the threat to their vital system of informants. They ordered a brutal crack-down.

"We have suffered more than any other village," a popular committee leader said eight months after the incident. "Electricity and phone lines were cut immediately. They still have not been restored. The first siege started the day the collaborator was killed and lasted 42 days. The first three days were a complete 24-hour curfew, enforced by 1,500 soldiers in our village. Then for the following 39 days, no one was allowed in or out of the village, and no food or fuel was allowed in."

Conditions were terrible, but the villagers' organization and roots in their land made it possible to evade some of the restrictions. People in Qabatiya became accustomed to the lack of electricity and telephones and such hardships never isolated Qabatiya from the intifada. Hand-sewn Palestinian flags hang from the dead electric lines, and freshly-painted graffiti supporting the PLO, the uprising, and the new Palestinian state appear nightly.

"In fact, we were able to leave Qabatiya whenever we needed to," a local leader said. "The location of our village helps as it is surrounded by 16 mountains, with only two valleys. We know all the secret ways through the mountains which, of course, the soldiers don't know.

"So while the siege was going on, I went out and met with Israeli Knesset members. I had lived inside Israel and knew how to reach them. I met with Tawfik Toubi, from Rakah, and another new member. There was a debate in the Knesset, and then it was referred to [Defense Minister Yitzhak] Rabin. Rabin claimed he didn't know anything about the conditions imposed in the siege, but it was finally ended soon after the Knesset debate.

"During the siege, we also called in the International Committee of the Red Cross, to publicize the conditions of the siege. They came, looked at the situation and said they could help. But they only offered food. We didn't need food then, we needed the siege to be ended. People here wanted political help."

The villagers of Qabatiya didn't need food from the Red Cross because of an extraordinary collective mobilization that enabled them to survive the siege's blockade. Even the village's shape, the stone and cinderblock houses stacked up against the hill, helped build Qabatiya's intifada.

"Our village is a mountain of houses, you see, so you can move between them without ever going into the streets. We could watch for soldiers without being seen, and move between the houses by just using ladders.

"Our standard of living here is different now; we can live for a long time just on bread and olive oil. We visited each other, we distributed flour and bread to those who didn't have enough. Ever since the siege began, we bake all our own bread. We have strong family and neighborhood ties, so we were able to move between houses even when the electricity was cut.

"Our self-sufficiency is even stronger now," the committee leader said. "The

shops stock only a few basic Israeli goods. Home economy is increasing. We're building small-scale cooperatives, just between groups of a few households, raising rabbits, chicken and vegetables. That is what we're concentrating on now. We have a tradition of a home-based economy in the village anyway, but the uprising has strengthened it.

"Committees were formed according to the needs of our people: a social committee to help the poor, an agricultural committee, etc. After the police resigned [in response to the UNLU's call in leaflets #9 and #10], we formed a guarding committee to prevent crime. They also coordinated with the *shebab* in protecting the village. During the first siege, there were rumors of settler attacks at night. The *shebab* spent the nights guarding the children, and making roadblocks; the settlers didn't come.

"We also would watch for soldiers from inside the village. The women played the main role in communications and watching for the soldiers, especially the old women. The young girls were with the *shebab*."

In early December, the majority of villagers were out picking the last of the year's olive harvest. Most of Qabatiya's residents are olive farmers, and the seven privately owned olive presses in the village were working in full swing. The atmosphere in the village was quiet, purposeful; the soldiers visible in the center of town seemed to have nothing to respond to. Wasn't Qabatiya a center of resistance?

"Before the olive harvest began, there were incidents here every day," one activist said. "Every day, there were demonstrations, stone-throwing, attacks on soldiers' buses. But we have imposed our own discipline now, because the economy of the whole village depends on getting the olives harvested. People accepted a decision that we would initiate no clashes during the harvest.

"Two soldiers tried to provoke a stone-throwing incident by pretending their car had broken down and that they were helpless. They tried to entice the *shebab* to attack them. But the young kids knew the rules, and just pushed their car out of town. Even our children know the economic realities, and won't provoke the soldiers during harvest time."

How long could such discipline last? "Oh, just till the end of the olive harvest, then the intifada will begin again. The harvest will probably be finished in about a week."

Eight days later, on December 10, the day after the first anniversary of the uprising, Qabatiya's youth again challenged the soldiers occupying their village.

"The uprising has brought many changes in the relations between all the people in the village," the popular committee representative said. "Now there is cooperation and support for the intifada from everyone. Class differences get blurred. Here, we don't have very rich and very poor people anyway; only small-scale businesses, and the unity is strong. Even the rich are nationalist, because the occupation affects everyone. The impact on the rich and the poor is different, but all are living under occupation.

"Israel doesn't have a role in our lives here now. You ask: where do the popular committees get their legality from? Certainly not from the occupation authorities. Within the laws of our Palestinian state, the committees are legal. In Jerusalem, Nablus, Ramallah, the popular committees confronted the soldiers. The people responded spontaneously, and the popular committees were born.

"I don't believe that every action, like Israel's occupation, has only an *equal* reaction. Sometimes the reaction, like the intifada, is much greater."

73

BEITA

In September, in the first year of the uprising, a mother-to-be from the village of Beita remained in prison. Munira Daoud, then eight months pregnant, is the sister of one of the two Palestinians from the village who were shot and killed by a settler on April 6, 1988. She is accused of throwing a stone at the man who had just murdered her brother. The Israeli settler who killed her brother, another young Beita man, and a teenaged Israeli girl in his charge, was not indicted for any crime. Munira Daoud's baby was born shortly after her release from prison; the baby died within a few days of birth.

The hillside village catapulted to international attention after what the villagers call "the incident." On that April morning, a group of teenagers from Elon Moreh, a nearby Israeli settlement, led by two armed settlers, came hiking across Beita's fields, trampling the new crops. Villagers asked them to leave, to avoid further damage to the fields. The Israelis refused, and some village children threw stones at them. Although no one was hit, one of the armed settlers, Rumain Aldubi, who had just completed a jail sentence and six-months-long banning from the area because of earlier provocative attacks against Arabs, immediately opened fire. He killed Musa Daoud Bani Shamsa, a 20-year-old Palestinian farmer who was working in the field. Other Beita farmers ran to protest the murder. Aldubi continued to fire, killing 19-year-old Hatem Fayez Ahmad al-Jabber, another villager. He continued firing, wounding at least two more Palestinians, and killing Tirza Porat, one of the settler girls. Beita residents reported that the girl had tried to stop Aldubi from shooting.

Initial Israeli press reports blamed the girl's death on a rock thrown by the Beita villagers, but within 24 hours the army admitted that she was killed by a bullet from the settler guard's gun. Despite this admission, the collective punishment of Beita continued. It even escalated. A few hours after the incident, Neal and I were held by Israeli soldiers at a roadblock outside Beita. From there, we could see the army helicopters, military vehicles and personnel, and carloads of settlers heading towards the village. In the next few hours and days, 24 houses were blown up by the military. More than 600 residents, including virtually every man between the ages of 15 and 60, were imprisoned, and six Beita residents were expelled from their lifelong home.

The Israeli Defense Forces had decided to make Beita an example. The whole village would be made to pay for the death of an Israeli girl at the hands of her own armed guard. Mass arrests, expulsions and destruction of olive trees continued for months. Beita remained under curfew for weeks after the incident, with reporters denied access to the village.

In the wake of this "special treatment," Beita remained steadfast; its resistance unyielding. The Palestinians call it a "liberated village," where Israeli soldiers often dare not enter.

Newly homeless Beita residents, forbidden by soldiers to rebuild or even to erect tents on the site of their demolished homes, ignored the military orders and put up the tents anyway. I saw an old man clearing the rubble to rebuild on his forbidden land. I stopped to ask him why he persisted in defying the soldiers. "We are Palestinians," he said. "We don't take orders from the Israelis."

Call #13 of the Unified Leadership of the Uprising, issued April 12th, paid homage to "Beita, the heroic Palestinian village." The UNLU called for April 13th to be "a day for collecting donations and solidarity with Beita, and for observing a moment of silence commemorating the martyrs of the uprising."

Neal and I visited Beita months later. The masked *shebab* had become the

main governing authority in the village. After a polite, but careful, inspection of our car and cameras by the young *molathemin* (those with covered faces), an older villager described to us how on previous occasions the search teams uncovered visitors, carrying American passports and claiming to be journalists, but with weapons hidden under back seats. That was the reason, they explained, why the *shebab* carry out their search "armed." Their weapons included an ancient sword, a small hatchet, and a homemade mace.

Later that night, a contingent of 15 *shebab*, in full, if unmatched, homemade uniforms, conducted military drills through the dark streets of the village. They were followed by about 50 young children, singing and chanting in support of the intifada and the PLO.

An older Beita resident, watching the disciplined march, said, "the *shebab* really are our government now. If there are problems between neighbors, any problems in the village at all, it's the *shebab* who solve them."

"It feels like the beginning of our own army now," another villager said, proud of the *shebab* and the uprising. "It's the beginning of our own army and the beginning of our Palestinian government."

BEIT SAHOUR

As the uprising has become a fact of life throughout occupied Palestine, it has taken different forms in different towns and villages. In Beit Sahour, a village of 10,000 adjoining Bethlehem, a combination of years of popular organization, and an educated and internationally connected population has meant a succession of constantly changing and creative resistance tactics.

Many of the cultural societies, women's committees, youth and workers' groups, began even before the Israeli occupation of 1967. The town's 30 to 40 neighborhoods, composed largely of extended family units, made organizing tight-knit and cohesive.

Before the uprising, villagers built alternative institutions designed simultaneously to challenge the occupation and to provide for people's needs. Later, the English-language *Jerusalem Post* described the town's resistance as "a quiet kind of uprising."

The "Beit Sahour Saga," written by local activists and academics, describes the development of "unarmed home guards protecting people and property; families planting backyard vegetable gardens; community lectures on first-aid; food, medicine and first-aid equipment gathered and stored; poor families given assistance; home schools opened to educate the children; and voluntary work teams trained to help clean the streets of Beit Sahour. At the same time, the doctors of Beit Sahour started a low-cost medical treatment program, merchants announced fixed and lowered prices for various goods, social societies and clubs raised funds to help the needy, and a group of professionals, including agricultural engineers, established an agricultural center."

That center, nicknamed "The Shed," opened on March 13, in the fourth month of the uprising. It quickly became a focal point of Beit Sahour's intifada. Spurred by the UNLU's call to build collective gardens, the center rapidly expanded from a volunteer network to hire a part-time staff. The organizers recruited dozens of agricultural professionals to provide advice to the community. The center provided Beit Sahour families with 200,000 vegetable seedlings, 150 kilograms of vegetable seeds, 1,000 fruit trees, 2,000 laying chickens, 2,000 frying chickens, pesticides, fertilizers and small-scale equipment. Larger equipment, including a tractor, was purchased and made available for community use.

As the center grew, it came under increased surveillance and harassment by Israeli soldiers. Deemed an illegal popular organization by the occupation authorities, The Shed was forcibly closed down on June 5th, 1988. Dr. Jad Isaac, its founder and a respected Beit Sahour leader, spent six months in administrative detention. He was released in November, 1988.

Beit Sahour's resistance has taken other forms as well. In this largely Christian town, the churches are key mobilization centers. A demonstration was organized on October 8, 1988, by women and children, demanding the release of three seriously ill Beit Sahour men and a woman six months pregnant, all held in administrative detention. Sixty or more women and a dozen children gathered in the courtyard of the Greek Orthodox church. They had decided they did not want a clash with soldiers that day; they wanted a dignified show of steadfastness.

Shortly, word of the vigil leaked out, and the church was soon surrounded by soldiers. A young woman carrying copies of the press statement was chased by a half-dozen soldiers with raised clubs. She managed to outrun them only by clambering over the rear wall of the churchyard and jumping to the steep ground 20 feet below.

The old women sat, talking quietly; the young women, fearless, taunted the soldiers. A few of the young women even pushed at the tear-gas cannister-loaded rifles. Efforts to negotiate with the soldiers failed. They refused to talk with the women, insisting that men from the village be brought in. Eventually, after a tense stand-off, the women and children were allowed to leave.

Every day, clashes erupt in Beit Sahour as soldiers attempt to force the villagers to paint over nationalist slogans that reappear each night, remove Palestinian flags, which fly again each day, and

77

attempt to collect taxes that Beit Sahour merchants resist as their contribution to the uprising. Curfews are imposed for weeks at a time. Attacks by settlers continue, especially on Beit Sahour's main road which is used by buses coming from T'kua, a near-by Israeli settlement. Cars have been smashed, Beit Sahour residents have been beaten up and bullets have been fired into windows of houses along the main road.

Several young men from Beit Sahour were killed in clashes. The first, Edmon Elias Ghanim, 17 years old, died when a granite stone was dropped on his head from an army lookout post on a five-story high roof. The march protesting his killing was broken up by soldiers, and a new curfew was imposed. When village residents attempted to pay condolence calls to the youth's family, the military responded by firing tear gas cannisters inside the crowded house.

In early December, 1988, only days before the first anniversary of the uprising, the women assembled in the church again.

This time, they came back to the church led by the mother, wife, and sister of Beit Sahour's most recent martyr, a young man who was shot and killed by soldiers in a clash in late November. For over an hour, they listened to the chanting of the Greek Orthodox Mass. Then they wrote, with their blood, messages to the world, asking women, especially, to help end the occupation. One document was addressed to the United Nations; the other to the Pope. Each was drafted in English and in Arabic, and each was signed in blood by the women and girls who filled the church.

One old woman, as she finished signing the appeals, cried out "we are not terrorists; we don't have tails. We want to feel that we are human beings. We are not animals, we are not birds to shoot. We want to save our children. That is the problem. We ask all the people in the world to help us, especially the women. Let every woman in the world put herself in our place and see her son when he is 20 or 18 or 16 and he has been killed. . . . [I signed the statement in blood] because I want to save my children. I will spill my blood and all the women here will spill their blood because we want to save our children, we want to save our young men."

"People here know the intifada will continue for a long time, without an immediate success," one Beit Sahour leader said. "It will continue because there is no alternative. We can't go back to the days before the uprising. It would be like committing suicide. We believe our struggle is to build an independent Palestinian state, with the leadership of the PLO. It will not be easy to change the occupation authority, but that is our direction. There is a connection between the PLO's diplomatic role and our work in the popular committees — they work outside, we work here.

"Our aim is to liberate our country. One way is through the popular committees. The PLO relies on information from our committees. We give them something to talk about in Geneva. Now there is dual power in the occupied territories, and one day our popular committees will reach up and challenge the occupation authorities."

"We're not against Jews, we're against Israel stealing our land, our water, our national independence. I'm not saying that we like the fact that Haifa, Yaffa, and our other cities, are now Israeli, but we have to be realistic. We have been dealing with them since 1967. It makes us start changing our mind and say there can be two states in this land.

"Our struggle is to have peace. This is called the land of peace, but for more than hundreds of years there has been no peace here. We want to reach the point where we can disagree but still have peace."

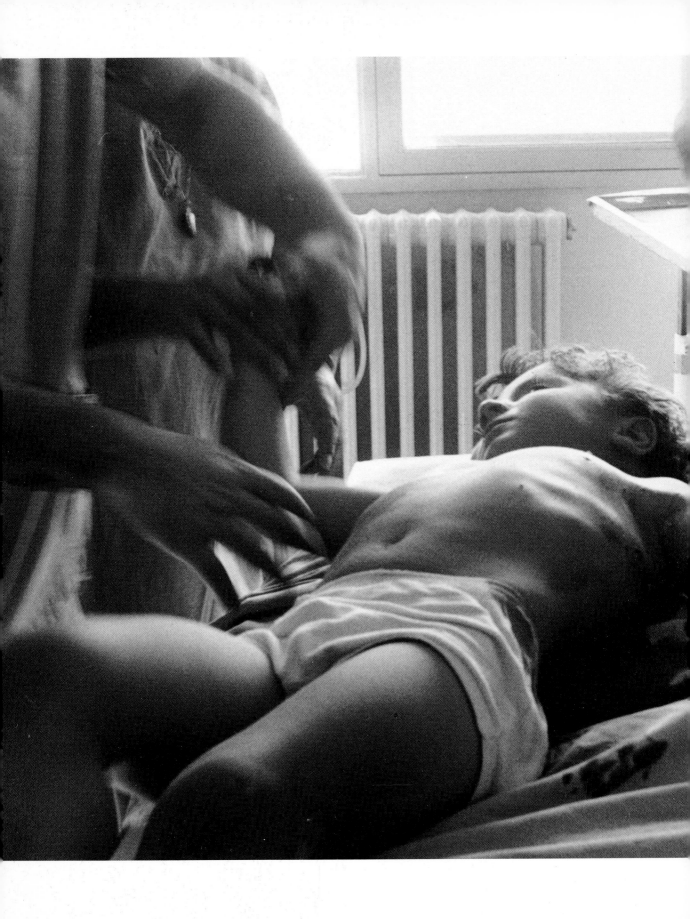

4. ◆ The Victims

The Palestinians living under occupation in the West Bank and Gaza Strip have paid, and are continuing to pay, a high price for the uprising. The militant, but unarmed resistance has been answered with Israeli bullets, lethal poison gases and sometimes fatal beatings.

Six months into the intifada, Amnesty International asked the question "why, when there are strict IDF [Israeli Defense Forces] guidelines on the use of ammunition, have so many civilians been shot and killed by members of the IDF, when some of them were not involved in violent demonstrations, and none of them had firearms?"

In January 1989, Amnesty went on to add that the organization "is gravely concerned that the Israeli authorities at a high level appear so far to have condoned if not encouraged the excessive use of force, knowing that it would result in the death or injury of thousands of people."

In the first 18 months of the uprising alone, according to the Chicago-based DataBase Project on Palestinian Human Rights, 650 Palestinians were killed by Israeli troops and settlers. Serious injuries receiving hospitalization or out-patient treatment exceeded 64,000. Forty-six Palestinians were expelled from their homeland, and 30 others are appealing expulsion orders. Approximately 6,500 were held as "administrative" detainees for renewable periods of up to six months at a time; about 50,000 more were arrested and charged or released. Over 100,000 olive and fruit trees were uprooted, as well as hundreds of thousands more seedlings and other plants. And over 917 buildings, mostly houses, were demolished or sealed, displacing an estimated 8,000 people from their homes.

The 1988 report of the National Lawyers Guild analyzes Israel's violations of the Geneva Convention protecting the rights of populations under occupation. Under Article 146, Israeli soldiers and officers should be held personally liable for "grave breaches" of the convention, to which Israel is a party. Article 147 defines those breaches to include killing, torture, inhuman treatment including beatings, expulsion, or willful deprivation of the right to a fair trial.

The aim of Israel's methods of suppressing the uprising is only partly to stop specific outbreaks of stone-throwing or tire-burning. According to Amnesty International, "several thousand Palestinians have been the victims of beatings, some particularly vicious, while in the hands of army and security personnel. In many instances, this was apparently intended to punish or intimidate."

Israeli efforts to suppress the intifada have included widespread collective punishment aimed at the entire population. Collective punishment is specifically forbidden by the 1949 Geneva Convention. Some Israeli tactics have been designed overtly for broad effect: curfews and sieges, in particular, amount to house arrest for hundreds, thousands, tens or even hundreds of thousands of Palestinians for days or weeks at a time. Declaration of closed military zones, where non-residents and the press are excluded from villages, camps, towns or neighborhoods, also deprives entire populations of the right to travel and the right to know.

But other kinds of treatment, initially appearing to be aimed at a single person, often blur the distinctions between individual and collective punishment. Hundreds of Palestinians, mostly teenagers and young adults, have been permanently maimed or paralyzed by Israeli bullets in the spine or brain, or vicious clubbings administered by soldiers.

When these young victims are first injured, they are heralded by their families and friends as heroes of the intifada — but the long-term reality they face is grim, and their families, indeed their whole communities, face the burdens of it together. There is a serious shortage of rehabilitation facilities throughout occupied Palestine, especially in Gaza. Only one rehabilitation-trained physician is available. The number of home-care providers is also completely insufficient.

Hospital officials in Gaza speak of keeping amputees and paraplegia victims longer than medically necessary, simply because there is nowhere for their patients to go for long-term rehabilitation care. This often causes shortages of critically needed beds during later emergency cases. At Al-Ittihad Hospital in Nablus, a senior physician described to us some of the intifada victims paralyzed with gunshot wounds. "Many of them are upstairs, here in the hospital. We don't have room for them here; this should be only for critical care, but we don't have any nursing homes. People in Ramallah applied for a permit to open a nursing home for these people, but the Israeli authorities denied the permit."

So, when a paralyzed young man, for example, leaves the hospital or coveted spot in a rehabilitation center and returns home, his entire family must redefine the contours of daily life to care for his personal needs. It may cost over $5,000 to install a wheelchair-accessible bathroom, for example, assuming he has a wheelchair available. That is beyond the reach of most Palestinian families, and for many, in the camps and most villages, the primitive plumbing and sewer systems simply are not adaptable. The result? The young man's family, friends and neighbors all must be permanently mobilized to move him to and from his bed, to feed, bathe and care for him. From the Israeli military's vantage point, the punishment goes far beyond one unfortunate young man — for as long as his wife, mother, father, sisters, brothers, neighbors are caring for him, they are that much less likely to be outside throwing stones, or organizing a vegetable cooperative, or teaching a popular education class.

At Bethlehem's Rehabilitation Center in late November, several patients were working out in the exercise room. Zuhriah Izzreke, a young woman from Beit Furik village, had been living in the center for four months. Her village was attacked by soldiers at 4 a.m. one morning. "We all came out to protest," she said, and 25 villagers were shot. "I was shot from 15 meters away with live ammunition. The bullet damaged my spine." She is now a quadriplegic, with virtually no feeling below her shoulders. Zuhriah is 19 years old.

Down the hall, Suleiman Taharia was trying on a new track suit brought by a journalist friend. He smiled as he pulled the pants over his left leg and the stump of what had been his right leg, amputated at the hip. He was shot outside his home in Silat al-Harithiya village near Jenin five months earlier; he had been living at the rahabilitation center since September. Suleiman doesn't say much; he spends much of his time drawing elaborate collages of Palestinian flags, doves of peace, and words and symbols of the Qur'an. Since his leg was amputated, he has embraced a militant Islam. Suleiman is 13 years old.

In Bani Naim village, not far from Bethlehem, a man, with exhaustion showing in his eyes, introduced Neal and I to his wife, who sat on a low cushion with her plaster-encased leg immobile in front of her. "It was during a 13-day curfew, and I was in front of my house," she said. "Soldiers kicked me, and then dropped a rock on my leg, and broke it." Her husband showed us a hospital release card indicating a fractured right tibia, the long shin bone. "She was in a cast and couldn't move for 45 days," her husband said, "then she got crutches. Now she crawls like a child around the house." Her husband, along with several neighbors, take turns caring for his wife and looking after their six children. "The soldiers yell at the children, frightening them. And I'm an Israeli citizen," he added quietly.

The collective punishment aspect is far more profound when the victim is a woman. The unequal division of labor around the home insures that a woman's injury or incapacitation or absence will be felt more immediately and more intensely.

When women began to be arrested and held as administrative detainees, new problems were created for extended families and communities. In the village of Beit Sahour, a happy event limned in stark relief the pain, both individual and collective, caused by Israeli use of administrative detention. When Habiba El-Atrash was arrested on September 6, 1988, she was four months pregnant. She was held in administrative detention for seven weeks. The night of her release, a joyous celebration rocked the el-Atrash house, as her six children, her neighbors, family and friends waited for her to arrive. After a series of almost farcical mix-ups, with her husband waiting outside the prison after she was already heading home in a taxi, shouts and tears of joy greeted her arrival. The festivities were relatively subdued only by the knowledge that the frequent army patrols would be alerted by too much noise.

While she was in prison, the other children were cared for by her mother-in-law. "My mother is very old," Habiba's husband said, "and the children are very active. It is hard for her to watch them while I am working."

The prisoners have become, in some ways, the symbol of Israel's inability to stop the intifada. Prisoners are picked up in sweeps or 4 a.m. raids, shipped off to Dahariyah prison or the notorious Ansar III prison camp in the Negev desert, and kept behind bars for six months detention, or wait for months for criminal charges to be announced. After six months of administrative detention, the term can be renewed for an additional six months. And again, and again. In the beginning of the uprising, only ranking commanders were authorized to impose administrative detention. By the third month, any Israeli military officer could issue wholesale orders for six months detention for any Palestinian — with no appeal, no judicial review, and no reprieve. By July 1989, the term for administrative detention had been extended to 12 months at a time.

An official of the Arab Journalists Association, released from six months detention in Ansar III in early October, described his time in prison. "There have been many random detentions, used against people with no relation to the resistance," he explained. "But those people now are rethinking their role. Now, they think that maybe they should be involved in the resistance, since they are being punished anyway."

He was arrested while at work in Ramallah, and taken to Dahariyah prison. "I told the soldiers I was a journalist," he said, "and in response two of them beat me unconscious. I was kept in Dahariyah for two days, and the treatment was very bad — there were beatings, all of that. Then I was taken to Ansar III. There, it was terrible. We saw no one from outside; we did not even see the Red Cross representatives for two months. There were problems with heat, bad and insufficient food, dirty water, snakes in the camp. Soldiers put me in a special room once, with my hands cuffed and my face in the sand, and I was beaten for two days."

The prison the Israelis call Ketsiot is a barbed wire compound in the middle of the desert. For the Palestinians who call it Ansar III, the name resonates with the history of earlier Israeli efforts to subdue those whose land it would occupy; its history looks back years before the intifada.

During Israel's 1982 invasion of Lebanon, a key goal was to destroy the complex system of PLO-led institutions that governed daily life for the hundreds of thousands of Palestinian exiles in Lebanon. That infrastructure, like the emerging UNLU-led popular organizations of the intifada in the West Bank and Gaza, threatened not Israeli security but Israeli control of Palestinian society. To accomplish that destruction, tens of thousands of Palestinians were arrested in massive sweeps of villages and towns throughout southern Lebanon. The men were held in a massive prison camp constructed in South Lebanon. It was called Ansar.

Four years later, escalating Israeli repression in Gaza led to a burgeoning prison population. Again, Tel Aviv responded by building a new barbed wire prison camp. This time, the prisoners were young Gaza men. Some of them, as young as 13, were held there for weeks or months and then suddenly, inexplicably, released. This camp, still operating at the time of the intifada, was called Ansar II.

Numerous reports from international legal and human rights organizations, including Amnesty International, Lawyers Committee for Human Rights, and others, and even Israeli lawyers and journalists, have described the harsh living conditions for prisoners at Ansar III. Insufficient water for drinking in the blistering desert sun, and virtually none for bathing; open, reeking excrement-filled holes for sanitation; no outside changes of clothes, or even underwear allowed, and washing of prison-issue clothes almost impossible because of water short-

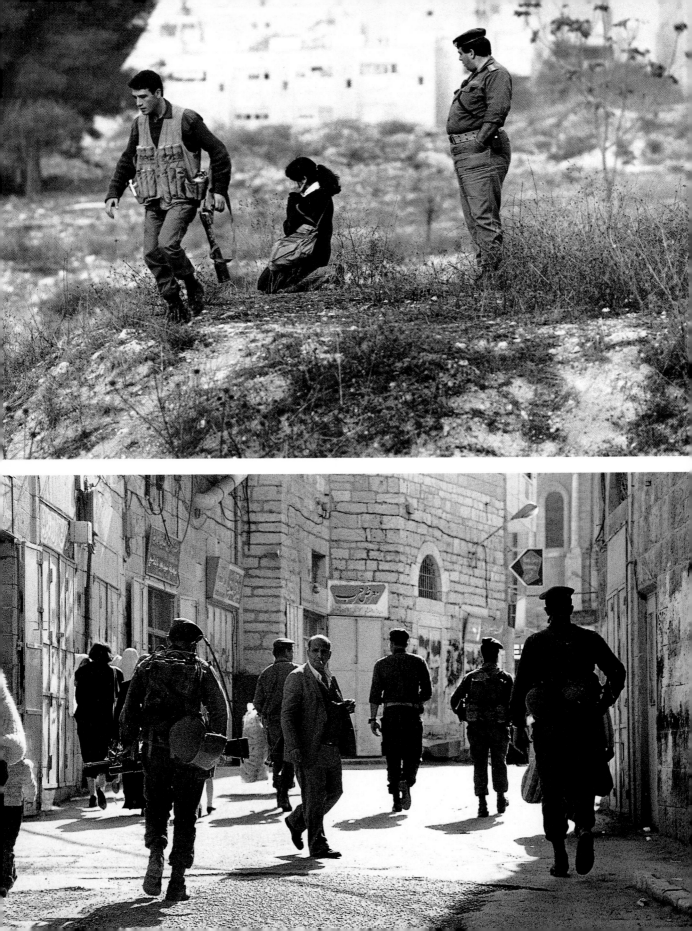

ages; insufficient and poor-quality food, leading to several outbreaks of food poisoning; lack of medical care, confirmed by arrested doctors, even for severely wounded or ill prisoners.

In December 1988, the New York-based Lawyers Committee for Human Rights issued a carefully documented report examining conditions in Ansar III. In their "Findings and Recommendations," they noted that "the detention of Palestinian residents of the West Bank and Gaza at Ketziot in Israel proper is a violation of the Fourth Geneva Convention. The Committee believes that the detention of Palestinian residents of the territories at this facility should not continue . . . The Committee is also greatly concerned by the accounts of collective and individual punishment, including physical mistreatment such as beatings and kicking, described in sworn affidavits by detainees at Ketziot."

The journalist-detainee told us that "food was kept in tents under the sun, there was no refrigeration. It was often spoiled or infested with insects. Nearly 400 prisoners were sick from food poisoning just in April; 150 of them were seriously ill, but they were only taken to the clinic, not to a hospital. The prison was completely closed during that time. For an entire week we had no visitors, not even lawyers — it was complete isolation."

But the barbaric physical conditions pale besides the daily abuse and humiliation facing Ansar III's inmates. According to the journalist, "prisoners were counted four times a day — at 6 a.m., 12 noon in the mid-day sun, evening, and midnight — and we would sit outside for 40 minutes for each count. We would sit, hands behind us, stand when our name is called, turn around and remain standing. Sometimes the whole thing was repeated. We asked the administration to reduce the counts, to cancel the noon and midnight counts,

but they refused to answer. . . . Prisoners were often beaten in front of other prisoners. We told the administration we could be made to be hungry or thirsty, but we would not give up our dignity. We asked just for the lowest range of rights, only those of the 1949 Geneva Convention, but even that was rejected. The administration said 'we only accept our own conventions, not those of Geneva.'"

He described the organization of the prisoners in Ansar III. "The unity of the prisoners is very strong. There are committees for keeping order, to distribute the food and for communicating with the prison administration. . . . All the prisoners share in the decision to declare a hunger strike; there's a discussion and then a vote. There were three strikes, for one, two, then three days. Part of the demands were to be told what the charges against us were. As we escalated the length of the hunger strikes, the response got worse. During the three-day strike, two prisoners were shot and killed, 10 others were wounded. The soldier who led the shooting was the commander of the prison guards. The prisoners wanted to issue a legal protest to the ICRC [International Committee of the Red Cross], but the soldiers wouldn't allow it, and started firing tear gas, and then shooting. Ibrahim Samoudi was killed. He was from Yamoun village near Tulkarem, 36 years old, married, and had two kids. The other one killed was Asad Showa, 30 years old, from Gaza. He was married too.

"We tried to discuss things with the prison administration, we tried to reach their human side. We demanded to be treated like prisoners in other countries. But the administration didn't accept or even answer our demands. They said they have limited instructions, their main aim is to humiliate the prisoners. 'Why else would we bring you here, if not to punish you?' they said. Some prisoners said to them that they know of the Israeli system of democracy, so why do you treat us like this? The guards' answer was 'democracy is just for Israelis — you are not included.'"

Speaking of those arrested because of the occupation he said, "we are the faithful Palestinians, with faith in the justice of our Palestinian cause. The occupation's repressive measures are aimed at destroying our will. It does not strengthen them, but it gives us strength to resist them and to emphasize our national demands. The Israeli authorities believe that mass detention of large numbers of people will stop the intifada. But they can't stop our will, and our demand for our rights, including our national rights, will continue. Giving us those rights is the only solution to the intifada."

Two months after his release, the journalist was arrested again, and returned to Ansar III for a second six-month term.

Somehow, the prisoners maintain their dignity through collective activity and resistance. Another journalist, who also spent six months in Ansar, described the prisoners' commitment to education. "Fourteen of the 224 men in our section couldn't read," he said, "so we taught them to read in the six months. Many of the rest of us studied foreign languages; there were classes every day in English, French and Hebrew. There were several academics there too, a PhD. in biology from Bethlehem University and others. They held classes in science, economics, political science; we journalists taught classes in history. Jail was really good for us — it's like a university. Even an Israeli official that came to Ansar III once said 'Ketsiot is a school for the PLO.' [Defence Minister] Rabin came to the prison too — he met with the prisoners, asked what they wanted. The prisoner committee said 'we just want to be treated like human beings, not like animals.' Rabin told them 'no, that's too political.'"

For Israel, the real problem with administrative detention is that when the term is over, unless it is renewed, the detainee goes home. And the return home for these graduates of this "school for the PLO" means the return to their village, camp or town as a popular hero, educated, politicized and re-mobilized through the long hours of quiet political discussions in the stifling tents of Ansar III. They return more committed than ever to resist the occupation.

On the Israeli side, study during the intifada did not mean languages or economics. Emphasis was on military matters, on dreaming up new weapons every month. One of the earliest, was the introduction of so-called "plastic" bullets, in fact made largely of metal and ceramic. Ostensibly less lethal than regular bullets, the new ammunition was supposed to be used only in tightly controlled situations. It was, according to Defense Minister Rabin, to be used only by specially trained marksmen, from more than 70 yards away, and aiming only at demonstrators' legs. On September 27, 1988, Rabin held a press conference to announce the policies limiting the use of these supposedly non-lethal bullets. The same day as the press conference, two of the three Palestinians killed in Gaza were shot by plastic bullets in the brain.

In the weeks leading to the first anniversary of the uprising, December 9, 1988, two more new weapons made their appearance. The effect of both, relative to quelling the intifada, was non-existent; the effect of both, relative to the bodies of young Palestinians, was horrific.

In Al-Makassad Hospital, in the week before the anniversary, a teenage boy from Kalandia refugee camp, north of Jerusalem, lay in bed. He had been shot at virtually point-blank range, only two meters distant, by an Israeli soldier whose rifle was loaded with the latest steel bullets. They are heavy metal spheres surrounded by a thin rubber coating. Each is about the size and weight of a large marble. Six of the new bullets hit him in the face. One penetrated his skull bone and remained there waiting for surgical removal. The other five had torn up the skin and muscle on the side of his face.

The second new weapon is even worse. Four young Palestinian shepherds from northern villages were hospitalized in November 1988. They were among the first 20 victims of what the Palestinians call the "exploding chocolate bars." The four had been seriously burned over 15 to 25% of their bodies from exploding fireball packets thrown by Israeli soldiers. The packets, covered with silver foil-like wrapping and about the size and shape of a candy bar, are engineered to withstand being handled and tossed around, but burst into flames when the wrapper is torn open.

One victim, age 20, said he saw the packet dropped from a helicopter over Tubas village; in near-by Tamoun, boys of nine and 15 said that one was tossed by a soldier driving by in a passing jeep. Majid Sub'hair Said, a 14-year-old from Qabatiya, spoke from his hospital bed. "I was in the camp outside the village with my sheep," he told us. "I saw the soldiers throw something, I didn't know what it was. There were about 10 soldiers in the patrol, and they kept walking after they threw it. I picked it up, and it looked like chocolate. It exploded when I tried to open it. Two of my sheep were killed in the explosion; the flames were about two meters across."

A senior physician, treating the boy at Al-Ittihad Hospital in Nablus, said, "I don't know exactly what it is — but the only thing I have ever heard of that is anything like this is napalm. We call these things mini-napalm bombs. We have never seen anything like this before."

Some of the anti-intifada weapons in Israel's arsenal are far more familiar; they have been in use since the uprising began. Two in particular have come to be viewed as part of day-to-day life during the intifada — although, despite their ubiquitousness, they continue to wreak a devastating toll. They are curfews and sieges.

The difference can be important. In a village or camp or town under siege, no one and nothing is allowed in or out of the area. Food and medical supplies are not allowed in, people cannot leave to go to their jobs outside, and journalists and other visitors are kept out. Inside the area, during at least part of the day, life can go on, in the profoundly abnormal way that passes for normalcy during the uprising.

During a curfew things get much worse. A curfew, in the parlance of the Israeli military, means a shoot-to-kill curfew. It means house arrest, for the entire population, and the constant threat of injury or death by trigger-happy soldiers on patrol, alert for anyone setting foot outside her or his door.

Just outside Al-Amari camp one windy October afternoon, Neal and I were examining the small-scale chicken and rabbit cooperative shared by half a dozen households next to the camp. Watching the hens peck for worms and stroking the baby rabbits, the scent of tear gas suddenly drifted over the four-meter high wall demarcating the camp. A static-filled amplified voice called out in Arabic, at first barely audible, then rising in a loud crescendo as the loudspeaker-equipped sound truck made its rounds through the camp. "What is it saying?" we asked, for the residents had not paid much attention to the voice.

One young man looked up from the rabbit cage. "They're warning the people they will be shot and killed if they come outside their houses," he said, almost casually. Al-Amari camp had been under 24-hour-a-day curfew at that time for 23 days.

In many instances curfews are imposed for days, even weeks at a time. A 15-day curfew imposed on Jabaliya camp in Gaza began in the first days of the uprising. In Qabatiya, 42 days of siege and curfew conditions followed the killing of a collaborator in response to his murder of a four-year-old village child. And in Beita, the death of an Israeli settler teenager was answered, along with arrests and six deportations, by a long curfew. That was followed by weeks of siege conditions during which journalists, gathered from around the world, were kept out of the village. This collective punishment was imposed despite the Israeli army's acknowledgement that the girl had been shot and killed by her own Israeli settler-guard.

In many cases curfews were imposed on a wholesale basis. Al-Haq/Law in the Service of Man's report on the first year of the uprising, *Punishing a Nation*, notes that "by January 13, 1988, the date on which all eight Gaza refugee camps were simultaneously put under a 10-day curfew, the 64,000 residents of Jabaliya had already spent 22 days under enforced confinement. The 13,000 inhabitants of Balata Refugee Camp near Nablus, where the uprising began in the West Bank, were under curfew for 26 out of these 35 days. By the end of the first month of the uprising, in excess of half a million residents of the occupied territories in approximately 20 separate locations had been under prolonged curfew. . . . Enforced mass confinement for extensive periods of time has become so routine that on November 7, 1988, in what constituted an advance notification of five days, the Israeli newspaper *Ha-Aretz* reported that the military government intended to place all Gaza refugee camps, and possibly Gaza City as well, under curfew from November 12–15. [This coincided with the meeting of the Palestine National Council in Algiers that declared an independent Palestinian state.] In fact, as Palestinians had widely been anticipating, the entire Gaza Strip, with an estimated population of 700,000, was placed under a total curfew 'until further notice' on the night of November 11. It was not lifted until the morning of the 17th, making it the longest blanket curfew on the Gaza Strip since the beginning of the occupation."

Gaza was not the only place for such harassment. Al-Haq notes that "Nablus, the largest city in the West Bank with a population of at least 100,000, spent more than 65, or approximately one out of every five days, under total curfew during the first year of the uprising. Prolonged curfews were imposed for periods of 10, 7 (twice), 6, 5, and 4 (twice) days. The nearby Balata refugee camp was under prolonged curfew for a total of more than 130 days during the same period. If one adds the shorter curfews, it is likely that this camp has been under curfew more often than not during the past year. . . . On November 15, 1988, the day that Palestinian statehood was proclaimed, the entire Gaza Strip, all West Bank refugee camps, all major towns and cities except for El-Bireh/Ramallah, El-Khalil (Hebron), and East Jerusalem, in addition to a number of villages were under curfew."

Somehow, Palestinians have managed to get used to living under house arrest with the threat of death just outside the door. Somehow, they manage to live a life that in some ways looks astonishingly normal. In Gaza, one April night, while visiting a Khan Yunis camp home, we said goodbye to neighbors preparing to leave shortly before the 10 p.m. curfew.

Camp residents told us that in Khan Yunis, like every other camp in Gaza and most in the West Bank, a curfew is in force every night. Every night, somewhere in the camp, soldiers raid houses — kick down the doors, arrest any men they find inside, beat and brutalize the women and children. Somewhere. Every night.

How do you live with that fear every night, I asked a young woman in the house while getting ready for bed, how can you sleep? "We're not afraid any more," she answered, "we have nothing more to lose." She drifted off at once and slept soundly until early morning. Throughout the night, soldiers were audible, calling out in Hebrew as they drove jeeps or walked foot patrols through the otherwise-silent alleyways of the camp. I was the only one in the house who spent much of the night listening for soldiers at the door.

Along with curfews and deportations, the form of punishment most immediately collective is the demolition of houses. Sanctioned under Israeli military law as a means of punishing "stonethrowers" and others deemed a challenge to the occupation, at least 497 buildings, almost all of them homes, were destroyed by the Israeli military during the first year of the intifada. In the small town of Jiftlik, for example, at least 100 homes of sharecroppers were demolished or burned in a single day.

Sometimes houses are destroyed as direct retribution for perceived acts of resistance. Others, as part of the broader process of land expropriation and Palestinian dislocation that have been part of the Israeli occupation since 1967 and before.

One collective demolition took place in Kesan village, a tiny hamlet in the hills north of Bethlehem. On November 23, 1988, four houses were demolished, displacing 67 people including 20 children under 10 years old. A year earlier, just before the intifada began, the villagers were notified that their land was forfeit — it was wanted for expansion of the nearby Ma'ale Amos settlement. "The soldiers told us they would move us to Tuqua, that we couldn't stay here" a local resident said, standing on the ruins of his demolished home. "But the army has no land to give,

the land in Tuqua has other owners."

The Kesan residents went to court. Their lawyer got a temporary order halting the demolition, and they thought everything was settled. But then, suddenly, "the soldiers came back, and gave us only five minutes notice before they began the demolitions. They came with 200 soldiers and three bulldozers — 30 army cars. They declared the village a closed military area, and prevented anyone from moving. The bulldozers destroyed the houses between 8 and 11:30 a.m. that day."

At the time the houses were destroyed, the families said they would stay on their land. The Al-Gazal family, one of the four, has a certificate for land ownership dating back to Ottoman times. The soldiers tried to stop them from putting up tents on the site of the destroyed buildings. "But the land is our right hand," the head of one family said, "we will not leave. We will stay here until they kill us."

Kesan is built high in the hills; it was cold in November, and the winter wind whipped across the flat plateau. One father looked around at the children, most of them sniffling with bad colds brought on by the cold nights unprotected by the canvas tents. "We are afraid the soldiers might come again; we do not expect any good from this government. Our children are cold and sick, and we have no medical care here. The settlement has a good clinic, but we can't go there — they would kill us. We have to go into Bethlehem."

"During the intifada, like any village in Palestine, there have been demonstrations here. . . . First, we must stay on our land. Second, we try to get a clinic here. Inshallah [God willing], our Palestinian state will happen. We want to live in freedom, as citizens with all our rights. . . ."

Is he sorry the intifada happened, because it has caused such problems for his family? "No, we are not sorry. If the intifada gives a good result, we will pay with everything we have. All we ask is that they give us our rights. We want to build a state. We want freedom and peace, on our own land in our own homes."

A few days later, four more houses were demolished in El-Khader, not far from Kesan. On December 7, 1988, 200 people from the surrounding towns and villages converged on the small village to protest the demolitions, and to visit each of the four families to express support and offer assistance.

An El-Khader leader spoke at one of the demolished homes during the march. "We want to express our feelings because the army and government of Israel destroyed these houses. We offer help for you to rebuild; the rebuilding is not for these families alone. These destroyed houses now are owned by all the people of Palestine. Israel can destroy, and throw down the stones of the building, but they cannot take the stones from our hands, our children's hands. All the Palestinian people, in Beit Sahour, El-Khader, Bethlehem and Beit Jala, all of the West Bank and Gaza Strip, feel with you. Our deep and best feelings are with you."

He explained later, "this visit gives all of us a high feeling. Everyone was there — Christians and Muslims, it's mostly Muslims now in El-Khader, and Christians in Beit Sahour. There is no difference in our land between Christians and Muslims. Religion is for doing good — this land, our country, is for all the people — Christians, Muslims, everybody. Islam says there is no difference between the religions, but people must live together in peace. But it must be peace with justice. The people who own the demolished houses, they haven't made any 'mistake,' haven't done anything wrong towards the government. Their 'mistake' is that they want freedom. Now we are without freedom, the

freedoms that other people in the world have. We agree for Israel to live beside our Palestinian state — that Yaffa, Lod, Haifa, we agree that they are Israel.

"The PLO now throws this to the world — the PLO is not terrorist. Yasir Arafat requests peace now. The PLO has changed, and Palestine has changed its society. The intifada changed opinion inside the PLO and in Israel. I hope there is a good result — it must be to establish a Palestinian state here. I hope — maybe time will create this state. . . . Yasir Arafat understood what the Palestinian people wanted. We hate to see the army here on our land, we hate how this life has become. We want peace, it is a necessity for us. We have finished what we have, it is finished. Our life now is like that of animals because of the occupation, it has dehumanized us."

In one particular example, the demolition of houses, and the Palestinian response to the demolition, gave new impetus to the resistance. The city of Nablus had been under 24-hours-a-day curfew for almost a week in early October. The days of curfew created a new reality in the city, for the local leadership of the uprising had used the time to consolidate a heightened level of resistance.

During the middle of the curfew period, the military demolished six houses and sealed four others with cement. They claimed that "suspected stonethrowers" lived in the houses. With the clear intent of intimidating as many Palestinians as possible, the demolition team entered Nablus accompanied by an Israeli television crew, and the early morning explosions were broadcast live. The 12 families who lived in the 10 houses were left homeless. One father pleaded in vain with the Israeli cameraman to film his small son crying "show this, show this — this is what you should show — where will this child sleep tonight?"

But the effort at intimidation backfired. The people of Nablus poured into the streets, defying the shoot-to-kill curfew, to express their outrage. Responding to the loudspeaker call of the local leadership of the uprising, the city's population succeeded in defying, if only for a short time and while still paying a high price in continuing casualties, the Israeli effort to suppress their intifada.

But what surpassed even that defiance was the collective action to find new homes for the families. Again the uprising leadership broadcast a call to defy the curfew, and this time, it was for a specific purpose. Again the call was answered, and hundreds of carpenters, electricians, plumbers, stoneworkers, painters and others congregated at the site of a half-completed building owned by a local trade union. It was intended to be an office building, but had been abandoned unfinished in the early months of the uprising. Within only 24 hours, the building structure was completed. The families moved into their new apartments the same day.

For some victims, Israel's intifada tactics mean a long-term, even permanent separation from their homes and families. These are the Palestinians expelled from occupied Palestine, faced once again with exile and loss of a homeland.

On October 9, 1988, Ruwayda Ma'ale, wife of 30-year-old Odeh Ma'ale, one of 25 Palestinians ordered expelled on August 17, 1988, led a contingent of Palestinian and Israeli Jewish women in a large protest against the deportations. The 3,000 to 4,000 demonstrators marched through Tel Aviv chanting in a mixture of Hebrew and Arabic: "Rabin, Rabin, yala' yala', tse miyad, mi Ramallah." Roughly translated, it is addressed to Defense Minister Yitzhak Rabin, saying come on, let's go, get out of Ramallah immediately.

After the march, Ruwayda Ma'ale explained why the Israelis are resorting to expulsion. "You know, after the Palestinian-Jordanian divorce, Israel [faced] two choices: either solve the problems with the Palestinians immediately in an international peace conference, or transfer the Palestinians so they could keep the land and force the Palestinians outside the area. Israel tried the second choice first, so she started with those 25 people, and she put them under order of deportation. Maybe it was to see the reaction to beginning the deportation process. They want to see the reaction both of Israeli and international public opinion, and also the Palestinian reaction."

Asked how she believes the Israelis are reacting to the deportations, Ma'ale replied, gesturing to the demonstrators massed in front of her, "as you see here, now we are standing with the Israelis who are against deportation. The left side [of Israeli politics] is becoming wider because of the deportation policy. They see it is so dangerous for their peace and for their state, much more than for the Palestinian peace and the Palestinian state."

Odeh Ma'ale's case was on appeal to the Israeli Supreme Court. "There is no decision yet," his wife said. "The decision may take until the middle of next month. . . . But look, we know that there is no justice in the Israeli courts. If there is justice, that means [they should] put a charge against him, and take him to court. But to give him an order of deportation, without any charges, that's a shame."

Can the deportation policy, and the threat to use it more, succeed in crushing the intifada? "No, surely no. The order deporting the 25 people, and the announcement of a new list of 15, maybe for 300 more, did not stop the intifada. The intifada is strong, strong and strong, more and more. The Palestinian people look for peace, they look for their state, peacefully. Things have changed a lot this year, we want to solve this peacefully, without war, without more blood."

Ruwayda Ma'ale's skepticism towards the Israeli court process is well-grounded. Those facing expulsion have no legal right to see the evidence on which the order is allegedly based, and in all the appeals of all the Palestinian expulsions, the High Court has yet to reverse a single one. In the summer of 1989, Odeh Ma'ale was expelled to Lebanon.

In a report released five weeks before the intifada began, the Israeli government's Landau Commission claimed that expulsion "has a considerable deterrent influence in restraining terrorist acts and hostile subversion." During the uprising, the stated intention was to expel those identified as leaders. On July 8, 1988, the military authorities announced the expulsion of 10 trade unionists, journalists, students and businessmen, claiming they were leaders of the uprising.

The National Lawyers Guild report documents how "expulsion violates Article 49(1) of the 1949 [Geneva] Convention, which states: 'Individual or mass forcible transfers, as well as deportations of protected persons from occupied territory to the territory of the Occupying Power or to that of any other country, occupied or not, are prohibited, regardless of their motive.'" The Israeli High Court's answer? The Geneva Convention is not applicable to Israel's occupation of Palestine.

Even the United States felt compelled to issue a formal protest to Tel Aviv after the announcement of the August expulsion orders against 25 Palestinians. The State Department said that "such harsh measures are unnecessary to maintain order," and charged that expulsions "had become the norm." The European Economic Community issued a similar statement, and the United Nations Security Council voted unanimously to condemn the expulsions — including a virtually unprecedented U.S. vote against its Israeli ally.

Akram Haniyeh was arrested two years before the intifada began. After 3 weeks in prison, he was expelled to Switzerland, and turned over to the International Committee of the Red Cross. He told me: "When I am alone at night, I always think about a Palestinian poet who died five years ago in a hotel room in London. His friends searched for five days to find a suitable place for him to be buried. Many Arab countries refused. I think many Palestinians living in exile think of that possibility. It is one reason we are searching for our rights. We want to live in our country. We want to have a place to live, and also a place to be buried in. We are struggling for a homeland, and also for a cemetery . . . a place to be buried."

For the Palestinians killed during the intifada, burial in Palestine, despite the occupation, has become a final act of resistance. The martyrs of the intifada are not only victims; each death sparks new steadfastness, each funeral becomes an act of collective resistance, each life becomes a talisman for those who continue.

A popular committee leader in Beit Sahour explained that "when we hear of new martyrs, people do not become weak, they become stronger, and ready to participate in the intifada. People are ready to sacrifice everything for the intifada. Palestine *is* the intifada now; we believe Palestine will be destroyed unless the intifada continues."

"Our martyrs," he said, "are the candles for people to move in the night."

The death of one small martyr, killed in Nablus on October 18, 1988, seemed to light up many such new candles of resistance. In Al-Ittihad Hospital that afternoon, I waited with a Palestinian colleague outside the operating theatre where surgeons were removing a plastic bullet from Neal's leg. He had

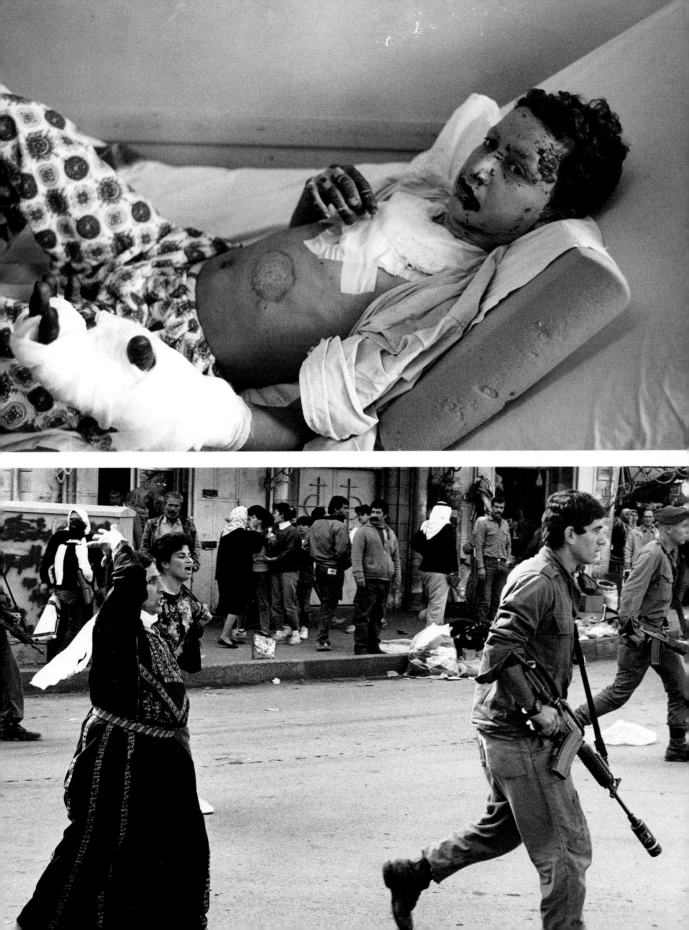

been shot by an Israeli soldier earlier in the day in the casbah, or old city, of Nablus, while photographing the soldiers on patrol.

While we waited, a man raced up the stairs into the surgery area, carrying a small child in his arms. The child was unconscious, and man and child both were drenched in blood. The Palestinian journalist and I grabbed Neal's cameras, and raced into the operating room after the child. Surgeons bent over the small senseless body as hospital technicians draped us in sterile gowns and shoved us toward the table.

The surgical team labored over the boy for almost six hours. The massive gunshot wounds caused traumatic injury to his liver, stomach, spleen and both lungs. In the end, their herculean efforts failed. Ziya Jihad Fayez Haj-Mohammad ultimately died from suffocation caused by his perforated lung aspirating particles of food from the sandwich the child was eating when he was shot.

Ziya Haj-Mohammad was five years old.

The photographs of the dying child, sped by wire to newspapers around the world, caused an uproar inside Israel. The English-language *Jerusalem Post* noted on October 20, 1988 that "the IDF [Israeli Defense Forces] senior commander has been concerned over the extensive international coverage given the shooting, and the worldwide distribution of a news photo of the dead boy."

A few days after the shooting an IDF public relations officer appeared on Israeli television. "I spoke with the father to apologize," he said. "We heard it was one or two bullets. I can say it was a wrong shot; they were shooting from a checkpoint 400 meters away."

In the days after the child's killing, his family's home on a hill above Nablus became a kind of shrine to the young martyr, and to the intifada. The courtyard of the building, and each landing of the stairway up to the family's sixth-floor apartment was filled with flowers, wreaths, flags, banners. They were signed by virtually every Palestinian organization: all the constituent groups of the PLO sent tributes, there were mementos from each of the women's organizations, from the leadership of the popular committee of Nablus, the committee from the family's own neighborhood, the Unified National Leadership of the Uprising itself. Inside the apartment, the walls were draped with more flags and banners, some sent by Ziya's young schoolmates, others by the *shebab* from the neighborhood guarding committee.

On a cold afternoon about a week after the boy's death, a group of children from his school came to pay their respects to Ziya's parents. Eight or 10 children entered the apartment, in military formation led by the oldest in their group, a small boy of about nine or 10 years old. The children's faces were covered, some with the black-and-white checked *kaffiyahs*, others with the full-face masks used by the *molathamin* of the villages, to hide the faces of the intifada's incognito activists.

The children conducted a short flag ceremony in the family's living room, then solemnly presented to Ziya's parents a Palestinian flag with a stenciled picture of Yasir Arafat on one side, and Arafat's deputy Abu Jihad, murdered by Israeli commandos at his home in Tunis in the fifth month of the uprising, on the other. They marched out silently. The youngest of these little *molathamin* was six years old.

Ziya's father, looking at a photograph of his small son's coffin, draped with a Palestinian flag, told me, "We need our rights, our own state; the Jews can live in their state also. We want to live in peace here, with the Jews. I hope Ziya will be the last martyr of our two nations, of Arabs and Jews. Then we can reach peace."

5. The Resistance

Few pictures have captured the imagination of the world as acutely as that of the "children of the stones," the youth who have challenged the Israeli army with little but stones and courage. While the Palestinians resisting the occupation remain militarily unarmed against bullets, gasses and demolition teams of the Israel Defense Forces (IDF), their militancy and fearlessness have effectively neutralized the army's ability to control the streets of occupied Palestine.

In the first days of the uprising, throwing stones at soldiers was part of the spontaneous reaction to the brutal, and intolerable occupation. There was no Palestinian army in the West Bank and Gaza Strip, and so stones, and later a few primitive molotov cocktails, were the only weapons available to resist the Israeli Defense Forces. Quickly, throwing stones against well-armed soldiers became both the norm and metaphor for the intifada.

But like other aspects of the uprising, stone-throwing soon lost its spontaneous character, and was absorbed into the multi-faceted organizations of the intifada. Virtually every sector of society was drawn in, including those whose age or inclination precluded direct involvement in the clashes. Vivid pictures abound, of old women in traditional embroidered dress, carrying trays of stones on their heads to supply the young hurlers.

Indeed, even the reliance on stones, the refusal to take up arms in self-defense, represents a collective decision, within the expanding unity of the PLO's internal and external wings. There is a wide-spread belief among Palestinians that only the weight of public opinion, Israeli and international, will prevent the Israeli army from moving in to essentially annihilate the Palestinian uprising through massive military assault and large-scale mass expulsions.

In *nida'a* #5, issued January 30, 1988, the Unified Leadership recognized that reality. "To the people of the uprising," they urged, "Let us chant in our demonstrations what daily reality has proven: 'Our masses know no fear . . . Their stone has become a kalashnikov.'" (In Arabic, the chant is rhythmic and popular during street actions.)

Given the intensity of Israel's military attacks on Palestinian camps and villages, what is astonishing is that the collective discipline has held, that individual Palestinians have not decided on their own to challenge Israeli bullets with bullets in return. For example, in the two days following the U.S. announcement that it would open talks with the PLO, Israel launched a savage military escalation in Nablus, resulting in eight deaths and dozens of serious injuries in the curfew-shut city on December 16 and 17, 1988. Many Palestinians believed that the increased assaults were consciously designed to provoke an armed Palestinian response, in a desperate effort to defend the beleaguered town, that would provide the Israelis an excuse to raise the level of military methods still further. But even that barrage of lethal entrapment failed to cause a break in popular acceptance of the no-weapons stricture.

But forsaking arms cannot be equated with avoiding militant challenge to the occupying army.

In Ramallah one October day, a demonstration was set for 11:00 a.m. The downtown commercial district, busy in the three hours before the 12 noon strike-decreed shop closing, was filled with customers, stores staffed with harried clerks. But somehow, everyone knew. No one spoke directly of what was afoot, but the air was thick with unspoken signals, with raised eyebrows and half-smiles.

Everyone walking the streets and in the stores pretended not to notice the growing numbers of young men gathering on the sidewalks, looking like window-shoppers or girl-watchers. No one paid attention to the gatherings of young women, strolling from store to store, not buying anything. Somehow, everyone knew.

At the stroke of 11, the demonstration began. Shopping bags disappeared, and suddenly the strollers, men and women alike, were transformed into masked *shebab*. The chanting began, and barricades were quickly built across the streets to block the soldiers' jeeps. Shopkeepers pulled closed their steel shutters, and would-be customers scattered to nearby side streets. There was concern, even agitation, but no panic.

Groups of demonstrators ran down the road toward the nearest military checkpoint, two blocks from the gathering point, shouting slogans against the occupation and in support of the PLO as they ran. One of the *shebab* acted as tactical traffic controller; he stood in the middle of the road as streams of demonstrators ran past him. At a certain point, when he judged the numbers right, he called for a halt by the protesters running towards the checkpoint, keeping one group back, dividing the protesters in two. No one challenged his instructions.

With a few words passed through the ranks, the demonstrators scattered. Some, mostly women, raced toward the small alleyways and side streets leading to the commercial center, heading for local construction sites filled with rocks and broken cement blocks. They carried the stones back toward the center of the street, where the rest of the men, presum-

ably better able to throw the stones, waited.

The soldiers sped toward the barricades, sirens blaring, and firing rubber bullets from their jeeps. They were met by a hail of stones that sent them back to their rooftop lookout post, only to be met by the rocks of the second group of *shebab* who had come in behind them. As is most often the case, no soldiers were hit. In their protective uniforms and helmets, behind the rock-proof screens of their jeeps, the occupying army remained unhurt. As the soldiers retreated, they began firing barrages of tear-gas at the demonstrators, then raced the jeeps back down the street.

The demonstrators vanished down the side streets, in ones and twos, or small groups of four or five. One group of five or six women, with a jeepload of soldiers uncomfortably close behind, ducked down an alley and climbed a low fence into a backyard garden. As a search patrol slowly moved past the house, a door opened from inside, and the women slipped inside the courtyard door. They remained there for a while, stripping off their *kaffiyahs*, and trying not to choke or cough too loudly from the remnants of the gas, until the soldiers had gone. The demonstration was over.

Twenty minutes after it began, groups of strollers, again with shopping bags and parcels in hand, were appearing throughout the downtown area. Shops reopened for the last 20 minutes before the noon strike. At some point in the confusion, a new Palestinian flag had been hung on an electric line. Another day in Ramallah's intifada.

But even with the large-scale participation of old women, merchants, and many other strata of Palestinian society in the resistance, it remains the youth and children who symbolize the intifada. Children's demonstrations, with most participants under the age of 12, have been savagely attacked by Israeli soldiers using clubs and tear gas. In the first year of the uprising, 20% of the deaths, or 87, were those of children 16 years and under; 30 were under the age of 10, and 26 infants between one day and three years old were killed by tear gas.

But the teenagers and children remain at the forefront of the resistance. An activist in Beit Sahour's Arab Women's Committee described how "in the first months of the intifada, we asked some three-year-old girls what they felt when they saw the soldiers. They said 'we're not afraid.' We asked them why, and these children said 'they are on our land, but they will leave because we will hit them with stones.' Our children know everything about the intifada; I am very proud of our children."

In the Dheisha refugee camp, one autumn afternoon, a young girl, 13 years old, sat shyly while we talked with her mother and her older brother who was recently released from administrative detention in Ansar III. But her shyness belied an impressive singing ability, and vanished when she was asked to perform. The song she chose was a new song; it spoke of resistance, of the intifada. "Down with fear, the people are no longer afraid," she sang. "The blood, the red blood, spreads over the floor. The blood will liberate our home, the blood will liberate all our people for revolution. The voices of all the people in the valleys, and in all the villages, cities and camps. This intifada is the climax for the Palestinians; there is no alternative to the intifada, there is nothing but the intifada, for people in the Gaza Strip and in the West Bank, in the Galilee and in the Jordan Valley."

The next verse went on, "These are the colors of the Palestinian flag: the red blood, the white birds, the black nights, and the green for leaves, these are the colors of the Palestinian flag. The occupation builds fences to keep the people in; we fight against the occupation's fences in order to get our rights, to win our victory. However the occupation builds those camps or fences, we will not give up the intifada, we will not forget our land."

After the first months of the uprising, the local activists in each town, village and camp had learned the ropes of resistance. Contention with the military authorities was increasingly carried out on terms set by the *shebab*, not by the soldiers. The demonstrations themselves serve two purposes: they provide an immediate, in-the-streets challenge to Israeli control of Palestinian territory; and they mobilize the Palestinian population with new confidence, strength and collective discipline.

During those first months, the highest percentage of casualties occurred during demonstrations, as large groups of young militants stood their ground against withering salvos of Israeli gas and bullets. But after about four months of experience, Palestinian tactics changed. Demonstrations still occurred, but they were smaller, more mobile. The *shebab* taunted soldiers or pelted army jeeps with rocks, but then dispersed quickly down muddy alleyways and over roofs and fences, in escape routes inaccessible to the heavily armed and motorized troops. Challenging the soldiers had not stopped, but the horrifying blood-price of large-scale, stationary demonstrations would no longer be paid.

After 21 years of occupation of the West Bank and Gaza Strip, young Palestinians armed with nothing but stones managed to seize the political and tactical initiative for the first time.

Increasingly, the Palestinians set the time, and the place, to demonstrate their power. In the isolated village of Sa'ir, one late November day, the local *shebab* planned a large march. They organized it carefully, quietly. They were determined that this action not lead to a clash with the soldiers; they wanted to prove to themselves and their own people their ability to control the streets of their occupied town.

But the Palestinians also wanted to demonstrate that ability to the world. So they carefully, quietly approached four journalists, one Palestinian and three foreign, to let them know when and where they could get a "hot" story. The journalists, Neal, two other photographers and a writer, agreed to keep advance word of the march a secret.

The reporters' cars were met at the entrance to the tiny hamlet of Shuyuk, in the hills above Sa'ir. Pre-assigned *shebab* took their car keys, and arranged to return the cars at the finishing point of the march. The demonstrators, over 100 young men with faces masked with checked *kaffiyahs*, each carried a red, green, white and black Palestinian flag as they marched in tight military formation. They chanted slogans in support of the PLO and the intifada, or counted cadence as they marched, weaving in and out of the streets of Shuyuk, gathering all the villagers as they went.

The children of the village joined in behind them, most of the adults following as well, as they wended their way down the hill to Sa'ir. Again, the chanting and marching in and out of the main square of the town brought the rest of the local population into the streets to join the mobilization. In the square, near the town well, the *shebab* gathered their supporters. A flag ceremony began the program, with Palestinian flags run up the flagpoles. Speeches were made, broadcast on a battery-run bullhorn. Then a large cassette player was connected to the bullhorn, and a group of the masked activists performed a *debka*, the traditional national dance of Palestine.

There were more speeches, music, and then the demonstration was over. Flags were taken down from the flagpoles, the flags carried by the marchers furled and stacked for future use. Neal and the other journalists were given back their car keys, and shown where their cars had been parked nearby. The *shebab* had transformed the streets of Sa'ir into a liberated zone for more than three hours. The soldiers never appeared.

Orchestrating such large-scale actions, unarmed but military-like in discipline, organization and secrecy, does not happen spontaneously. In virtually every village, camp, and neighborhood of the larger towns, resistance committees function parallel to, but separate from, the local popular committees. Along with planning demonstrations, these groups, mostly men between 16 and 28 years old, have the responsibility to act as guards to protect villagers, especially the very old and the very young, from military or settler attacks. Every village and camp has an elaborate warning system, based on whistle signals. The signals notify residents of soldiers on patrol, or an impending settler assault, sometimes even just a stranger arriving in town. The warnings mobilize the youth to come into the streets to protect the village, and also notify those young men on the run from the soldiers to leave the village and head up to their hilltop hiding places.

In almost every village, certain young men, and sometimes a few women, have been identified by the Israeli occupation authorities, or by Palestinian collaborators, as leaders of the intifada. Perhaps the military believes someone is a member of a popular committee, or coordinator of the underground popular school. Maybe a woman is believed to head up one of the women's committees, or a doctor has been teaching too many first-aid classes.

Whether the Israeli assessment is accurate or not, the person named must choose between risking arrest, or setting up hiding places in the surrounding countryside.

For many young people, especially in the villages of the West Bank's north-

ern hills, this means relying on hidden caves used as refuge to escape from the soldiers. The village youths spent their childhood days climbing the hills, and are intimately familiar with the land and its hiding places. On the run from soldiers, these "wanted" activists now spend their days as shepherds or farmers, working with their families in the villages, but at night they retreat to candlelit caves, stocked with blankets, water and a bit of food, to avoid capture.

In the village of Qabatiya, a young man described his months on the run. "Soldiers came to my house to arrest me," he said. "They never said why. But I escaped. Then for four or five months I came home during the day but left at night to sleep in the hills. While I was hiding, soldiers often came to my parents' house to search for me. I could stay in any safe place, but I couldn't stay twice in the same place in the town."

"Finally soldiers came one day and warned my mother they would demolish the house if I didn't surrender. So finally I surrendered. After two nights in jail the soldiers told me they didn't want me to surrender, because they wanted to destroy my home. But this way my home was safe — I spent five months in administrative detention."

A key task of the resistance committees is to serve as organizers and tacticians of the almost daily challenges to the soldiers of the occupation. And during the daily challenges, it is these young *shebab*, most often functioning as masked *molathamin*, who are the shock troops of the Palestinians — and who pay the heaviest price.

The resistance committees, sometimes called strike forces or strike committees, evolved like other sectors of the uprising, from spontaneous formation in response to immediate needs, to a more formal and coordinated structure. Significantly, especially given the primacy Israel attaches to stopping the street demonstrations and imprisoning their organizers, these local groups have managed to construct a sophisticated network of resistance committees on city-wide, regional, and national levels.

The national leadership of the resistance committees publish their own newsletter, called "Conscience of the Uprising." Written, typeset, and printed underground, the publication addresses both specific issues of concern to the strike committees themselves, as well as questions more broadly affecting the Palestinian resistance. Like the *nida'at* of the Unified National Leadership of the Uprising, the pamphlets of the national strike committee are distributed clandestinely, appearing suddenly, overnight, on street corners, stairwells and sidewalks throughout occupied Palestine.

The fourth issue of the newsletter, which appeared in October of the first year of the uprising, featured articles by and for the strike committees: "People's Creativity in Forms of Resistance," "For Higher Levels of Organization," "Let's Make Better Forms of Popular Struggle Against the Enemy," "What Is Required Is Raising the Level of the Offensive" and "Letter to Members of the Popular Resistance Committees."

While the organizing of direct resistance is a task somewhat distinct from the broader responsibilities of the popular committees, the street challenge to Israel's military cannot be completely separated from the political goals of the intifada. The strike committee's publication focuses squarely on this intersection of direct resistance inside Palestine, with the international political and diplomatic initiative the uprising has made possible. Two articles in the 10 page pamphlet, for example, examined political questions facing the Palestinian movement as a whole, including the PLO's external leadership: "It's Time to Get Out of the Camp David Period," and, aimed specifically at influencing the upcoming Algiers meeting of the Palestine National Council, "Organizational and Political Tasks for the PNC." Still other pieces analyzed the situation of, and provided extra encouragement and support for, specific areas or towns of occupied Palestine: "For Our People in Gaza," "For People in the Capital of Our Independent State — Jerusalem."

The intifada's resistance is not limited to direct confrontations with Israel's occupying army. A key component of the uprising, one that has provided much of the payoff in terms of changing political conditions, has been the economic resistance. The tactics have been diverse and creative, pulling into active motion, or at least acquiescent acceptance, virtually the entire Palestinian population. Part of the economic intifada has focused on creating alternative economic institutions, including agricultural and production cooperatives, community gardens and volunteer agricultural work. But more direct resistance tactics include a boycott of non-essential Israeli goods, widespread commercial and labor strikes, the creation of merchants' committees, and tax resistance.

The call to stop buying Israeli goods emerged very early in the intifada, based on a widespread recognition of the importance of the West Bank and Gaza as Israel's largest export market. *Nida'a #3* of the Unified Leadership, issued January 18, 1988, called on "our people of all sectors and classes: Let us begin today boycotting the Israeli goods for which an alternative is produced in our national products and factories, specifically such products as chocolates, dairy items and cigarettes." A week later, on January 24, *nida'a #4* linked the growing boycott with alternative production: "Honorable nationalists . . . we call on you to join us in the following: concentrating all energy on cultivating the land, achieving maximal self-sufficiency aimed at boycotting the enemy's goods."

By confining the boycott to those Israeli-made items which either were unnecessary luxury goods or had existing national replacements, the UNLU ensured a much higher level of collective participation in the boycott. It also left room to escalate the demands placed on the Palestinian population as the intifada matured and the people's political understanding and willingness to sacrifice expanded.

In this, the boycott call was matched by the terms of the far-reaching commercial strike. From the beginning, the widespread closure of Palestinian businesses came to symbolize the intifada. The merchants themselves, in alliance with the popular committees and the UNLU, formed committees to set the terms of the strike. They recognized that the people could not survive, over the long haul, without certain basic goods and services, and that the effort to build local self-sufficiency was a long one.

Accordingly, shops were not immediately closed in a full general strike. Openings were set at three hours a day, generally from 9 a.m. till noon. Even that was flexibly administered, allowing, for example, much longer hours in the smallest towns with insufficient grocery stores to serve people working in distant fields. And the 21 hours-per-day closing order was specifically exempted for necessary businesses: bakeries, pharmacies, taxis, medical and legal offices all remain on regular, or more often expanded hours. Pharmacies and in some areas bakeries, in fact, rotate among themselves to ensure that essential medicines and bread are available 24 hours a day.

But while the UNLU recognized the public's need for certain commodities, it remains committed to raising the level of the Palestinians' ability — and will — to sacrifice for the uprising, to learn to survive without many kinds of goods. General strikes, in which all commercial enterprises, except pharmacies,

remain closed for one or two, even three days at a time, have been part of the intifada's arsenal of economic weapons from the beginning. The frequency and duration of strikes has been increasing, as the UNLU leadership trains the people to endure drastic reductions in the Palestinian standard of living.

In the very first Call, issued January 8, 1988, the UNLU began a tradition of expressing encouragement and congratulations to their people for their accomplishments in the intifada, while simultaneously raising the ante of future tactics. *Nida'a #1* called on "all sectors of our heroic people everywhere to abide by the call for a general strike on January 11th, to continue until the evening of January 13th. The strike is to include all private and public commercial affairs, Palestinian workers and public transport. The general strike should be observed exactly. The strike slogan will be 'Down with the Occupation — Long Live Free Arab Palestine.' . . . To our brothers, the owners of commercial stores and groceries: You must observe totally the general strike days. Your past observance of the strike was the most marvelous example of solidarity and sacrifice for the sake of making successful the stance of our heroic people. We shall do our best to protect the interests of honorable merchants against the revenge of the occupiers, and we warn against listening to the occupation's hirelings who try to make you open your stores. . . ."

By the fourth month of the intifada, the 21 hour daily commercial strike had become routine. Palestinians had learned to rearrange their daily schedules to accommodate fewer shopping hours, and to rearrange their family's clothing, food, and lifestyle habits to reflect scarcer availability of goods.

But by that time, the commercial strikes had also become a serious thorn in Israel's side. While not endangering Israeli security, the strikes and consumer boycott jeopardized Israel's economy by the loss of its most important market, and Israel's claims of controlling the people living under occupation. The economic clout of the commercial strikes, and the collective political empowerment the strikes provided for the Palestinian population as a whole, played crucial roles in building Israeli-Palestinian dual power in the occupied territories.

In Ramallah, for example, a large and wealthy market town, the battle over store closures raged for weeks. It was a battle for political control, between occupied and occupier. This round, the Palestinians won.

"When the strikes began," a local resident said, "the merchants would all close their shops at noon every day. After a couple of weeks, the soldiers came and announced that all the stores must close in the mornings, and open instead in the afternoons, from noon till three o'clock. That would have violated the strike rules, so the merchants refused. The soldiers threatened to arrest the store owners, but they still wouldn't open their stores after 12.

"After a few days of this kind of verbal stand-off, the soldiers came one morning and forcibly closed the shops. They did a lot of damage, breaking things and destroying food and other things in the stores. So the merchants announced that they would remain closed, that the strike would be in effect 24 hours a day. The only things for sale were bread and fruit from pushcarts in the street. That way the merchants themselves still were in control of the strike.

"But then the soldiers started going through town with crowbars in the afternoons, breaking the locks on the steel doors that cover the shops, and forcing open the doors. The shopkeepers responded by leaving their shops, and just going home. The shops stayed open, many of them, with no one in them and with all the goods just lying there in plain

sight. But you know, not a single thing was stolen. A few of the local locksmiths went around each night and rebuilt the locks on the doors, and then they would be broken by the soldiers again the next day. That went on for days. Finally, the soldiers gave up. It took several weeks, all told, but eventually we won the battle to control our own stores."

The merchants' organizations quickly became important bastions of the uprising; their participation ensured that the intifada was in fact a truly national, cross-class phenomenon, not simply the work of the most impoverished layers of Palestinian society.

One organizer of the merchants' committee described it as a "comprehensive organization, based in Nablus, to cover the whole of the West Bank and Gaza too. Before the intifada, the Arab Chamber of Commerce was the only group of merchants, and it was based only among the rich store owners. The ACC was formed under Jordanian rule, and it was linked to Jordan's political life. Individual officers of the Chamber were appointed by Jordan, based on their allegiance to the monarchy and in fact on their opposition to Palestinian nationalism.

"Since 1967," he went on, "Israeli attacks began against the entire Palestinian population. So the Arab Chamber of Commerce had to defend itself against those attacks, to protect its own economic interests. After the occupation, authority was transferred [from Jordan] to Israel. Nationalist merchants asked the Israeli occupation authorities to allow elections in the ACC, but Israel refused. . . . Then nationalist merchants began to organize in connection with the PLO, in all spheres to oppose the occupation. When stores were closed by the Israeli occupation authorities, for example, they would provide legal support and publicity.

"After the intifada began, the na-

111

tionalist merchants became more organized. They took more initiative, especially in response to the UNLU's calls. It's always hard to mobilize merchants because of their class, so it was a big achievement to build the merchants' committee. Agreement on strike hours was a major accomplishment. Early in the intifada, the army would force stores open, and the merchants' committee formed a watch committee to guard against looting. In Ramallah, the merchants' committee won the battle of the strike hours after a weeks-long battle in the spring. The blacksmiths would make new locks, glaziers fit shattered windows with new glass, everyone cooperated. . . . The committee has not felt that the sacrifices of the uprising are too great, because they are contributing to national goals. Merchants with losses due to fire, teargas, or other attacks get compensated out of a general fund. And the PLO has a welfare committee to help pay for those kind of personal and property losses."

This official of the merchants' committee was arrested following a Jerusalem press conference on February 2, 1988, which announced the work of the committee. He and another colleague were held for six months administrative detention. In early October, he was arrested again and held for 10 days. On November 15, the day of Palestine's Declaration of Independence, he was arrested for the third time, and released after six days.

Besides organizing merchants to support the intifada, the uprising has encouraged an entirely new kind of merchant to thrive. In the West Bank village of Kufr Nameh, a founder of the local grocery cooperative described the origins and work of his small store. "We began with 30 members of our cooperative," he said. "Each contributed $100. We started in 1985; we focused on selling national [Palestinian-produced] products, but there were only a few kinds of items accessible.

Our purpose was to make groceries available for low prices; our cooperative forced other shops in the village to lower their prices too. We sell all basic food and school supplies; during olive-picking season, we also sell plastic sacks.

"During the intifada, consumption in general is less, but it still takes the same work to keep our store open. There's a higher demand now for national products, and there are more available. For example, we sell all the products made by the Beitello Women's Production Cooperative. The population of our village is about 2,500 to 3,000; about 40% shop at our co-op, the rest at the eight other stores. When we first opened, the other shopkeepers didn't like it, but they couldn't really complain.

"People are more united now during the intifada. We have a popular committee, an education committee, food storage and distribution committees. The guarding committee is made up of kids with whistles; when they signal, all the people go into the streets. We have popular education classes for three hours a day, for all ages up through high school — but it's very difficult, and we have fewer kids now. Only about 60% of the village kids are in popular education.

"The soldiers are often in our village; they have stolen 10 cars, made numerous arrests. There are Palestinian flags, always flying. The army can enter, but it can't stop the education work, it usually can't find wanted people to arrest them. . . . The military calls this a 'closed area,' but it's a different story inside the village. This is a liberated zone."

On the nearby wall of the almost-destroyed bus station, damaged in a soldiers' attack, a painted slogan reads "Kufr Nameh will continue to burn in the intifada's sky."

The leadership of the uprising understood, from the beginning, that to succeed in moving toward an indepen-

113

dent Palestinian state, they must sever the complex web of political, economic, social and administrative ties linking Palestinian life to the Israeli authorities. A key part of that web is in the form of taxes. Throughout the years of occupation, Israel levied steep taxes against the Palestinians. It held the use of even part of that money, supposedly devoted to improvements in roads, health care, etc., hostage to "good behavior" from its occupied population. So, from the beginning, the UNLU emphasized the critical importance of tax resistance to the consolidation of the intifada.

In *nida'a #2*, the list of interim demands of the uprising included the "repeal of the arbitrary taxes imposed on the merchants." A week later, Call #3 spelled out in more detail what that meant: "To the heroic shopkeepers: You have taken honorable militant positions facing the occupation authorities' daily oppression; . . . we ask you to also continue forming and expanding merchants' committees in every street, city, village and camp. We ask you to prepare a unified plan, to be adopted nationally, for total abstention from paying the Value Added Tax (VAT). Whatever the occupation authorities' threats and measures, they will not succeed in stopping you, nor our masses and national movement, from realizing this slogan. Boycotting the payment of taxes is an essential slogan of our people's heroic uprising."

Escalating further, in *nida'a #5* "the Unified National Leadership calls upon all merchants to prepare themselves to fight the battle of boycotting the payment of Value Added Taxes soon. You should raise one slogan: 'No to the occupation, no to the VAT.' All of you should be prepared to burn the tax account books. The Unified National Leadership and your committees are organizing the battle everyplace in the occupied territories. We will declare the zero hour in a call soon."

By Call #10, issued March 11, 1988, the UNLU had determined that the political preparation for the no-payment of VAT campaign had achieved widespread popular support, and it strengthened and made non-negotiable the demand: "We call again on our heroic masses not to pay taxes. The Arab accountants must not deal with taxes. Our steadfast merchants should not hand over their tax accounts. The popular and merchants' committees will follow this matter, and the strike forces will punish those who do not respond to this call."

In practice, there was little need for coercion, for the no-payment call was met with enthusiasm. On December 9, 1988, the first anniversary of the intifada, a group of six merchants from Bir Zeit village were released from jail. They had been arrested two days earlier, in a sweep of the village merchants. The economy of the village had been brought to a virtual standstill because of the closure of Bir Zeit University, whose students, faculty and workers provide the main customers of the local stores. The university, like others in the West Bank and Gaza, had been ordered closed since the beginning of the uprising.

"They took us because of income taxes," one merchant explained. "They told me I had to pay 600 JDs [about $1,800]. They took 35 of us shopkeepers, but only six of us went to jail, the others they let go. You can't compare our income taxes with those in Tel Aviv — partly because our income is so much lower, but especially because we don't get any services from the government in return for the tax money.

"They took us in handcuffs to the tax office in Ramallah. We told them we had no money to pay the taxes. We said they must open Bir Zeit University so the stores could make a living. I have a small shop, I sell all kinds of goods. But with Bir Zeit closed, the shops here have no business. Without the university, just

114

one shop would be enough for our whole village.

"They tried to make a deal with us at the jail in Ramallah. They told us that the merchants they hadn't taken, who were still outside, had paid their taxes, so we should too. We knew it wasn't true, because we knew they didn't have the money either. They had just sent the other merchants home after checking their ID papers.

"In the jail, we said we would not deal with them, we would not pay them any money. We told them we were ready to go to jail for six months, because we don't make 600 JDs even in six months anyway. The soldier told us he has to pay 3,300 shekels [about $1,980] in taxes, but we said 'look what you get — medical insurance, health, all those things.' When my daughter was hurt, I took her to Hadassah Hospital; they wouldn't treat her until I found the money, because I have no insurance.

"We will fight by stones to get our own government. I feel bad to see the young kids in jail — there were two, age 13 and 15, in jail with us for throwing stones, but it's part of our struggle. The main problem here in Bir Zeit is taxes. They are much too high. More than half the population of this village now lives outside Palestine, so we depend on the students to buy from us. It's hard enough with the commercial strike, when we are only open for three hours a day, but without the students, it's impossible. There just isn't enough money.

"When we have a [Palestinian] government, I will pay taxes. I will get schools, hospitals, all those things in return. They [the Israelis] say they are ruling here according to Jordanian law, but before 1967 there were no taxes like this. They are coming for taxes from poor people — coming with machine guns to collect taxes. Taxes? On what income? I am ready to come out of the jail or go back to the jail, but I am not ready to pay

115

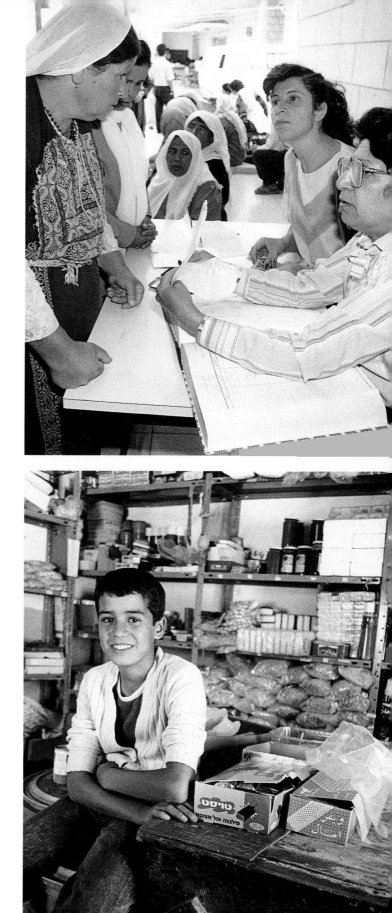

their taxes. I want self-determination for my kids, for the future. We want a Palestinian state, we want self-determination. My family has been in Bir Zeit for 500 or 600 years; we are not refugees, this is our country."

In some ways, the tax resistance is already laying the foundations for just that kind of Palestinian government. While calling on shopkeepers and others to refuse to pay Israeli taxes, the UNLU decreed a kind of Palestinian tax. It was designed to insure that those hit hardest by unemployment, imprisonment of breadwinners, house demolitions, etc., could be supported by the community. The funds would come from those whose economic status remained relatively stable. In *nida'a #29*, for example, calls to increase tax resistance is matched by the "call [to] the popular committees in all places to form national levy committees to collect donations from merchants, factories, employees and academics who have not suffered harm in order to achieve social solidarity during the uprising."

For the leadership of the intifada, each of the separate forms of resistance, whether stoning soldiers, refusing to pay taxes, creating alternative governing institutions, popular education — all are part of building toward a much broader, deeper campaign they call national disobedience: A crusade to complete the severing of Palestinian life from the control of the Israeli occupation, a crusade which will match economic resistance with direct challenging of soldiers, the boycott of Israeli goods with the creation of Palestinian alternatives, transforming longstanding assumptions about social relations into new understandings of a new kind of Palestine and a new kind of Palestinian.

Nida'a #13, issued April 12, 1988, analyzed the intifada's steps in building the national disobedience campaign. It said: "We have begun to see its implemen-

tation as the apparatus of the 'civil administration' dissolves. The majority of employees have resigned, such as those working in the police, customs and taxes. A large number of the appointed municipal and village councils have resigned. The great majority of our people have abstained from paying taxes. The boycott of Israeli goods has been tangibly realized. Our workers have abstained from going to work in the Zionist projects [settlements]. Other achievements include the increasing spirit of cooperation and solidarity among our people, as well as the return to cultivating the land. The concept of self-sufficiency has spread in practice, and the popular committees have spread in all the occupied homeland. Our people have begun creating a new national lifestyle and consolidated their national authority."

A popular committee leader in El Bireh described his vision of national disobedience. "On the political level, it means a full boycott of the occupation apparatus, including the civil administration and all departments of administrative control. Economically, workers will refuse to work in the settlements and in Israeli factories. We also must end the consumerist economy, build a more spartan lifestyle, create cooperative alternatives. Organizationally, the popular committees will take on real authority. And on the resistance level, we must escalate via our strike forces, resistance committees, as well as getting support from the PLO from outside.

"We are concerned about the stage of national disobedience. Higher sacrifices will be demanded, and discussions about it are already increasing. We need plans for partial, then total disobedience — partial means two or three weeks on full strike, with no work, then we resume a period of regular activities for a while. We can't move toward a total campaign yet, because the preconditions include outside financial support, and that is still difficult in this period.

"The popular committees play a key role in building toward the national disobedience campaign, to help us reach that new stage. We encourage local traditions of storing food. We collect money for distribution to the poor. We're also increasing home economy, destroying Israel's effort to create a consumer society deeply dependent on Israeli goods. The more costly the occupation is for them, in economic, political and human terms, the sooner Israel will come to the negotiating table.

"We don't have the conditions yet for face-to-face, one-on-one negotiations with Israel. In an international peace conference, with the PLO on an equal footing, we could hold all sides accountable. But now, direct negotiations with Israel would favor the side of the enemy. . . . Israel is stronger technologically, economically, politically and militarily, and it has support from the United States. Palestinians want peace, but it's not yet in our hands. . . . We are creating future guarantees in the nucleus of the intifada; all Palestinian capabilities are being mobilized. If the intifada were over, the experience in only one person could recreate the whole experience. The uprising has already laid the basis for the continuation of our people's struggle for liberation."

The numbered *nida'at* of the Unified National Leadership of the Uprising both chronicle and lead the progress of the intifada. The consistency of their appearance, suddenly, overnight, on the streets of Palestinian towns, villages and camps, provides an important psychological, as well as political reassurance. It shows that the leadership remains intact, that the unity still holds, that Israeli efforts and claims of capturing the leaders have not succeeded.

Since Call #5, almost every *nida'a* begins with the declaration that "No voice is louder than the voice of the uprising; no voice is louder than the voice of the people of Palestine, the people of the PLO." It reasserts the importance of the Unified National Leadership of the Uprising as an expression of Palestinian unity, and rebuffs efforts (most often Israeli but sometimes Islamic) to split or undermine its role.

The form of the *nida'at* also provide an effective means for the UNLU to raise the level of sacrifice and commitment it demands from the people it represents. By appearing every two weeks or so, new demands can be articulated, and initial responses to earlier calls can be assessed, praised or corrected. The Calls also serve as a vehicle for analyzing the broader national, regional and international situation; each begins with an update of political events in Palestine and in the world, and examines them relative to the progress of the intifada. Sometimes the uprising-related accomplishments of specific camps or villages are praised. Then the tactics for the next week can be outlined in the context of long-range political goals.

So, *nida'a #2*, issued only a month after the uprising began, called for "deepening the revolutionary essence displayed by our masses in the camps of Jabaliya, Balata, Askar, Mughazi, Bureij, Kalandia, Amari, Rafah, Khan Yunis, Shatta, Tulkarem, and in every Palestinian camp, village and city that are united in the daily struggle. . . . To the Cubs [Palestinian boys' clubs] and youth of Palestine, to the stone-throwers: Surely the neofascists will be forced to recognize the realities which your uprising has imposed, clearly indicating the way toward national independence, and raising the Palestinian flag over the sacred walls of Jerusalem."

The call went on to outline, for the first time, the interim demands of the UNLU, while "affirm[ing] the continuity of all forms of struggle under the PLO's banner until achieving our people's noble

117

goals of return, self-determination and the establishment of an independent Palestinian state under its leadership."

The interim goals, identified as "the uprising's direct and basic slogans" included "an end to the iron fist policy and the immediate repeal of the Emergency Laws and all deportation orders. Forbidding the violation of the holy places, and deporting the terrorist [former Defense Minister Ariel] Sharon from the Old City of Jerusalem. Withdrawal of the army from the cities, camps and villages, and forbidding its provocative practices and its opening fire on our unarmed people. Dissolving the village, camp and municipal councils and committees appointed by the occupation authorities, and implementing democratic village and municipal elections in the West Bank and Gaza Strip. Immediate release of all those detained during the uprising, and closure of the detention centers of Al Fara'a, Ansar II, Ansar III and Dhariyeh. Repeal of the arbitrary taxes imposed on the merchants. Stopping land confiscation, settlement-building and the settlers' provocations. Ending raids and closures of mass, unionist and educational institutions; ending the occupation authorities' interference in their internal affairs."

Some nine months later, interim demands were reasserted, drawn in sharper relief. In *nida'a* #27, issued October 9, 1988, the UNLU took the opportunity to "congratulate the U.N. Secretary General and all peoples who are supporting our rights. We confirm the necessity of achieving the following legitimate demands: 1) withdrawal of the occupation troops from Palestinian residential areas; 2) annulling all decrees of the occupation and [British] Mandate, and the Emergency Laws [legalizing administrative detention and deportation]; 3) stopping the policy of settlement-building and annexation, and removing the existing settlements; 4) releasing all those detained during the uprising, and closing the mili-

118

tary detention centers; and 5) international protection for the unarmed Palestinian people for an interim period of not more than a few months, in preparation for our people to establish an independent state with Jerusalem as its capital."

In early August, after King Hussein's dramatic announcement that Jordan would sever its administrative and financial ties to the West Bank, *nida'a #23* noted that "in fact, the Jordanian measures dissolving the legal and administrative ties with the West Bank, are among the most important achievements of the great popular uprising. They are a complementary step fulfilling the decisions of the Algiers Summit and consolidating the PLO's position as the sole legitimate representative of the Palestinian people; and the only party authorized to assume responsibility for them, in the homeland or in exile."

Five days after PLO Chairman Yasir Arafat declared the independence of the state of Palestine, *nida'a #29* spoke "To our proud masses: Your uprising is approaching its first year. It has achieved a new, glorious victory with the declaration of an independent Palestinian state by the leadership of the revolution, the PLO. . . . In order to materialize this decision [to declare the state], there should be more steadfastness and confrontation; all forms of struggle should be escalated. . . .

"There is no doubt that the declaration of an independent state will be a great moral and material motivation, pushing our people's struggle forward. The enemy's hopes and illusions that the Declaration would cause splits in our ranks, will be shattered. You, sacrificing people, have matured, as has your readiness to make more sacrifices and escalate the uprising. Today, you say there is no difference between Likud and Labor; both are repressing and killing our people in the occupied territories and in Lebanon.

We will continue to confront the new Likud era. Countering the Likud and Labor slogan of 'no concessions,' we will raise the slogan of 'no stopping, no retreat, and no surrender,' and 'yes to everything that will advance our march and achieve our independent state.' Yes to escalating the struggle until ending all links with the enemy, continuing gradual civil disobedience until reaching total national disobedience.

"There will be four more years of the rule of the most racist and extremist trends in Israel. But this does not scare us. Our people are determined to continue the struggle until the enemy is forced to yield to our will, and we achieve our legitimate national rights to repatriation, self-determination, and achieving the sovereignty and freedom of the independent Palestinian state."

6. The Results

Eighteen months into the intifada, a doctor from one of the popular health committees told me how "this new generation, that grew up during the occupation, they have now said they would not wait any longer. It used to be a question in the rest of the world whether we Palestinians even had the right to talk about freedom; now we have a new kind of self-respect. The intifada has brought an earthquake to our society. . . ."

The results of this earthquake, this "shaking loose," can be seen on both the internal and international levels.

Palestinians living under occupation, living the intifada, claim credit for the changing international conditions and the growing acceptance throughout the world of Palestine as a national entity. They see those changes as a direct result of the strength of the uprising itself.

The international shifts are easier to see and quantify. They began during the summer of 1988, eight months into the intifada, and they first emerged visibly within the Arab world.

In that first summer of the uprising, Jordan's King Hussein severed all administrative and economic ties with the West Bank. Hussein described the cutting of ties as an expression of support for Palestinian independence and the PLO. For the Palestinians, his act represented a crucial victory for the intifada, derailing longstanding Jordanian efforts to act as interlocutor for the Palestinians in any international arena.

Jordan's dramatic shift took place over the course of a single week. It began on July 28, 1988, when Hussein announced his abandonment of the $1.3 billion "condominium plan," linking Jordan with Israel and the United States to provide funds ostensibly to raise the standard of living of West Bank Palestinians. Two days later, Hussein dissolved the lower house of the Jordanian parliament, half of whose 60 members represented pre-1967 West Bank constituencies. On August 4, 1988, the king announced an end to the $50 million annual subsidy Jordan had been paying to a network of teachers, hospital workers, schools and other institutions in the West Bank.

These economic and political moves were highlighted by a major speech delivered by King Hussein on August 2, 1988, declaring that "Jordan is not Palestine," and endorsing the Palestinian call for an independent state. For Palestinians living under occupation and fighting for independence, it was a sweet victory.

"It was the intifada that forced Hussein to end relations with the West Bank," a Palestinian trade union member said, "not his own tactical ideas. He was obliged to cut the ties, to stop trying to act as our representative — especially with the United States. If he didn't, the intifada might have spread to Jordan too."

The next visible international accomplishment came three and a half months later. The Palestine National Council, the legislative and highest branch of the Palestinian national movement, convened in Algiers. Its extraordinary session acted on behalf of the entire Palestinian people, those living inside occupied Palestine and those living in scattered exile.

With the unanimous support of the delegates, and the power of the intifada behind him, PLO Chairman Yasir Arafat declared that, "in exercise by the Palestinian people of its right to self-determination, political independence, and sovereignty over its territory, the Palestine National Council, in the name of God, and in the name of the Palestinian Arab people, hereby proclaims the establishment of the State of Palestine on our Palestinian territory with its capital Jerusalem." A thunderous ovation welcomed Arafat's reading of the Declaration of Independence, written by Palestine's national poet, Mahmoud Darwish.

Speaking immediately after Arafat, Algerian Foreign Minister Boulan Balsaih announced that his country would be the first to formally recognize the new State of Palestine. The joyous session concluded with a uniformed band playing the Palestinian national anthem, as the new state's familiar flag was unfurled on the wall of the conference hall.

Outside the hall, the chants, songs and impromptu *debka* dances of celebration did not entirely hide a quiet undercurrent of sadness. Palestinian martyrs, past and future, could not be forgotten. The name of Abu Jihad, Arafat's deputy who was killed by Israeli commandos in April 1988, was repeatedly invoked as an example of the martyrs who had already fallen, as well as of those who will surely fall in the future as the intifada continues.

There was also a sober recognition of the long and difficult battles that still lie ahead. Nayef Hawatmeh, leader of the Democratic Front for the Liberation of Palestine, and part of the PLO's consensus bloc, spoke quietly the day after the Declaration. "If we retreat we shall be destroyed," he said. "We remember Sabra and Shatila, when those with the weapons left, when the forces of the Palestinian people left Beirut, and our people had no self-defense. Our people in the occupied territories remember well Sabra and Shatila. . . . Our only option is to continue the intifada, to suffer more and more . . . until we achieve victory."

Everyone at the Algiers meeting recognized how the intifada was creating new realities in the decades-old struggle for an independent Palestinian state. One of the most important of these new realities was the strengthened level of unity that the intifada had created throughout Palestinian society and throughout the PLO.

Dr. George Habash, a pediatrician who leads the Popular Front for the Liberation of Palestine, described the role of the uprising in this process. His organization, while disagreeing with certain aspects of the political program decided on in Algiers, viewed PLO unity as principal and accepted the majority vote. Speaking only hours after the Declaration of Independence, Habash said, "the intifada has forced us — and I'm glad it has forced us — to stay inside the PLO Executive Committee even with the differences we still have."

Referring to a popular long-time PLO slogan he continued, "we must say not only 'Revolution Until Victory,' but also 'Unity Until Victory.'"

In the days following the Declaration of Independence, countries throughout the world upgraded the status of PLO offices to embassies, and extended partial or full diplomatic status to the newly formed state. By late spring of 1989, 89 countries had recognized the State of Palestine.

The announcement of the new state sparked the beginning of a modest but important international realignment on the question of Israel and Palestine. Israel was increasingly isolated in the international arena. In December 1988, even the United States cast a virtually unprecedented vote against its Israeli ally's practice of expelling Palestinians from their home, resulting in a unanimous United Nations condemnation of Israel.

123

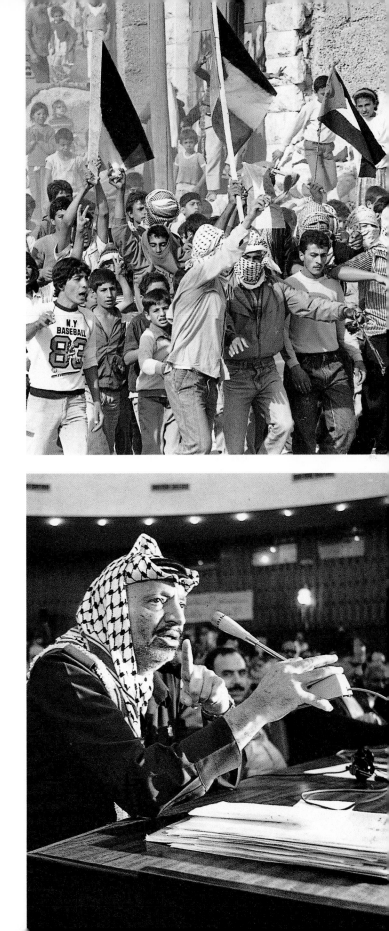

There were other significant gains registered by the Palestinians. The European Economic Community developed a unified position strongly supporting an international peace conference under United Nations auspices. The Soviet Union launched a wide-ranging effort to move the international community closer to convening such a peace conference. During a high-profile visit to a number of Middle Eastern capitals, Soviet Foreign Minister Eduard Shevardnadze said "it is our profound conviction that favorable prerequisites are now in place for movement toward convening an international peace conference."

The PLO's own peace initiative was further articulated by Chairman Arafat in December 1988 in Geneva, where the United Nations convened in a special session. The unusual location was mandated because the United States refused to give Arafat a visa to address the General Assembly at its regular headquarters in New York.

In Geneva, the PLO chairman clarified further the reality of the Palestinian search for peace with justice. Elaborating on the political program decided by the PNC in Algiers, Arafat called again for an international peace conference under the auspices of the United Nations Security Council. The peace conference, he said, would include "the permanent members of the Council and all parties to the conflict in the region, including, on an equal footing, the Palestine Liberation Organization, the sole legitimate representative of the Palestinian people."

"The PLO," Arafat went on, "will seek a comprehensive settlement among the parties concerned in the Arab-Israeli conflict, including the State of Palestine, Israel and other neighbors, within the framework of the international conference for peace in the Middle East, on the basis of [United Nations] Resolutions 242 and 338 and so as to guarantee equality and the balance of interests, especially our people's rights in freedom and national independence, and respect the right to exist in peace and security for all."

The language was careful, and Arafat's Geneva speech had in fact been voted on by the entire PLO Executive Committee. At his Algiers press conference the day before the Declaration of Independence, Arafat had reiterated that "our desire for peace is a strategy, and not an interim tactic. We are committed to peace, come what may. . . . We want peace." He repeated it again. "We want peace. We are committed to peace." And again, "we are committed to peace. We want to live in our Palestinian state, and let live."

For the United States, the relentless pressure of the intifada, now articulated in the PLO's diplomatic initiative, finally forced a long overdue political response. Within hours of Arafat's Geneva speech reiterating Palestinian intentions, Secretary of State George Shultz, acting through Swedish intermediaries, announced plans to open formal United States talks with the PLO. The announcement marked the end of the United States policy, developed by then-Secretary of State Henry Kissinger in 1975, to refuse to negotiate with the Palestinian organization. An era was ending.

The earlier era was not over yet; the State of Palestine had not yet taken official shape on the ground. But inside occupied Palestine, the outlines were already clear. A West Bank doctor, speaking in the eighteenth month of the intifada described how much of the State of Palestine is already real: "Now for the first time at night," he said, "I feel like I live in Palestine; that I live in my streets, my house. The *shebab* are our militia, our police. And we offer still to negotiate all of this, to negotiate for only a quarter of the country we once had. We are giving

125

up some of the rights of our future for a part of our present."

And so, while the world's attention was riveted on the dramatic events taking place in Algiers, Geneva, New York and elsewhere, equally striking changes were going on, quietly, inside Palestinian society. For many Palestinians, the overriding importance of the intifada is rooted in its impact on their own society, inside their culture and their world.

A trade unionist, in the second summer of the intifada, said that "the internal Palestinian factor is the most important part of the uprising — achieving changes in our society, inside Palestine. The international changes are important. The Soviet Union can push the U.S. to recognize those new realities, but the real changes must start on the ground."

The intifada led to a new kind of empowerment. The process of opening up a society often closed by old traditions, has expanded to include the PLO itself, and the organization's relationship to the Palestinians living under occupation. Suleiman Najab, leader of the Palestine Communist Party, described in Geneva how the intifada had strengthened the unity of the PLO: "Now we have been made accountable to our West Bank and Gaza supporters, not to the Arab countries," he said. "The intifada gave us the push forward. Now the Unified National Leadership of the Uprising, who we have named the Field Command of the Palestinian people . . . have shown that as long as we are fighting for the same goals, there is no danger of splits. Our unity has been deepened and strengthened."

Palestinian singer Mustafa al-Kurds, whose intifada music circulates semi-clandestinely on tape throughout occupied Palestine, brought the same thought to his poetry: "You, the people of the camps," he sings, "you hold us to our oaths."

The West Bank doctor explained how "the intifada is changing how people look at each other, everything about how we live. We are forgetting about empty slogans. People are more cooperative, more loving and respectful of each other. This is why we understand that our love for our country is more than just the land, but that our country is its people. . . . That is why we want to build this infrastructure, like a state, for our intifada. We need grassroots institutions to support our long efforts. This struggle will not be short. But they [The Israeli authorities] cannot jail a whole nation."

Five months after PLO Chairman — now Palestinian President— Arafat read the Declaration of Independence, Hanan Mikhail Ashrawi visited the United States. She is the Dean of the Faculty of Arts at Bir Zeit University, closed by the Israelis since before the beginning of the uprising. Ashrawi played a key role during the summer of 1988 in the influential U.S. television series, "Nightline in the Holy Land," in which she participated in a number of discussions and debates with other Palestinian and Israeli Jewish panelists.

Ashrawi delivered the keynote address to the Washington convention of the American-Arab Anti-Discrimination Committee. "The intifada's pride is the pride of a people who have forged national unity in the searing kiln of determination and sacrifice," she said, "welding together a oneness of purpose, a oneness of being, and a holistic vision of peace and justice. The health of our nation, the integrity of its identity, and the authenticity of its fabric are all indivisible from its collective commitment to the intifada as a self-generating, self-sustaining act of rejuvenation and pride. . . .

"Our rights are not to be reduced to mere 'legitimate political rights,'" she went on, "for we clearly claim and proclaim those universal rights of all nations

126

which no colonial or occupying power can eradicate. We claim our birthright and the truth of our vision, for the intifada is our national epiphany, and the inevitable birth of our state is its fulfillment.

"We stand in awe of the moment, in humility before the Palestinian people's collective endeavor, guided by the ethos of reconciliation and moral rectification which has given substance to this expression of humanity and peace. The intifada's humility is that of a nation which has reached deep into its innermost reserves of endurance and strength, and brought forth into the light a genuine vision and definitive values. The intifada's humility is that of the collective recognition of the power inherent in unanimity, in the equal sharing of risk and responsibility, and in the comprehensive involvement in state-building from within.

"It is with a sense of wonder and humility that we have scaled the wall of fear that the occupation had erected to try to block our vision. Now we have discovered vast expanses of promise and potential on the horizon, and with that discovery, we have gained self-knowledge. . . .

"We have committed ourselves to a light-filled life, denying the sun to no one, claiming what is ours without depriving others of what is theirs, building a future without destroying the past, and healing wounds which were not of our making. . . .

"For once, the authentic resonance of the Palestinian voice has filled the world's ears. It does not seek to silence others, but it will not be silenced, nor deflected. If, in this, we offend some well-intentioned friends who genuinely believe that they know what is good for us, or who think that our manner of articulation and our perceptions and concerns are not entirely identical to those which they aspire to convey or achieve, we would like to assure them that we understand that peace is the sum total of all its different, but harmonious, components."

It is the sum total of those components of peace that make up the terrible beauty of Palestine's intifada.

Photo Captions

■ Cover

Deir Ammar, April 1988.

■ p. iv & v

Kesan, November 1988. A group of Palestinian children climb on top of the rubble where their home used to stand. Two days earlier Israeli soldiers had demolished the house.

■ p. x

Khan Yunis refugee camp, April 1988. A small boy with his father.

■ p. xiv

(top) Portrait of a young Palestinian.

(bottom) Sa'ir, November 1988. Demonstrators, led by the masked *shebab*, march through the village unseen by Israeli soldiers.

■ p. xv

(top) Khan Yunis refugee camp, April 1988. A mother encourages her shy son to welcome visitors.

(bottom) Al-Khader, November 1988. A man sits in the ruins of his home, holding a photograph of his house before it was demolished by Israeli troops the day before.

■ p. 16

Jerusalem, December 1988. Soldiers threatening to arrest a Palestinian journalist during a demonstration.

■ p. 17

(top) Jerusalem, December 10, 1988. The day after the first anniversary of the intifada, schoolgirls confront the occupying troops.

(bottom) Jerusalem, December 1988. A girl runs through a cloud of tear gas to confront occupation soldiers.

■ p. 20 & 21

Jerusalem, December 1988. A young girl avoids the stare of the heavily armed soldier patrolling her streets.

■ p. 25   (top)   Jabaliya refugee camp, December 1988. A woman describes the demolition of her home by Israeli troops.

         (bottom)   Yatta, December 1988. The most recent martyrs are eulogized with a call to follow their example. The two young men were assassinated by an Israeli death squad.

■ p. 26 & 27   Deir Ammar, April 1988: Three generations of Palestinians.

■ p. 29   (top, left)   Khan Yunis, April 1988. Young girl in refugee camp.

         (top, right)   Qabatiya, November 1988. The morning after their wedding day, a couple sit for a picture; the bride's hands are stained with henna patterns.

         (bottom)   Beita, November 1988. The parents and older brother of a 13-year-old boy shot and killed the day before while fleeing Israeli soldiers.

■ p. 30   (top)   Beita, November 1988. At the boys' grave, the women of the village mourn.

         (bottom)   Beit Sahour, November 1988. Israeli soldiers break up a gathering of Palestinian women and children at the Greek Orthodox churchyard.

■ p. 35   (top)   Jerusalem, December 1988. A teenaged Palestinian girl is arrested by Israeli Border Patrol officers.

         (bottom)   Dheisha refugee camp, November 1988. A 13-year-old girl sings of the intifada.

■ p. 36   (top)   Tel Aviv, October 1988. Palestinian and Israeli women demonstrate together to demand an end to expulsions of Palestinians.

         (bottom)   Khan Yunis refugee camp, April 1988. Preparing breakfast. The bruise on the boy's left cheek is from a rubber bullet that barely missed his eye.

■ p. 38   (top)   Jerusalem, April 1988. At 12:00 noon throughout the West Bank and Gaza Strip, shop doors are shut as the daily commercial strike begins.

(bottom)   Jerusalem, April 1988. Unemployed Palestinians at informal labor market waiting for Israeli contractors to select them for low-paid day jobs inside the Green Line.

■ p. 43   (top)   Ramallah, December 1988. Demonstration commemorating the first anniversary of the intifada. It was broken up moments later by soldiers firing rubber bullets and tear gas.

(bottom)   Bethlehem, October 1988. Occupation soldiers in routine check of Palestinian identity cards.

■ p. 44   (top)   Jiftlik, November 1988. A small boy waits to be seen by doctors from a mobile clinic.

(bottom)   Silwan, December 1988. An Israeli soldier questions a small boy about who burned a tire.

■ p. 45   (top)   Beita, November 1988. A child peers out from behind his mother's shawl during a village funeral of a 13-year-old boy who had been killed by an Israeli soldier.

(bottom)   Beitunia, October 1988. A sidewalk memorial at the spot where the young Nidal Rabadi fell by the fatal bullet of an Israeli sharpshooter. Fresh flowers had been left there on the day which would have marked the boy's 16th birthday. The sign in Arabic reads, "Born in Jerusalem, October 8, 1972, killed in Jerusalem, July 19, 1988." The sign describes Rabadi as "Jerusalem's bridegroom."

■ p. 46   (top)   Bethlehem, October 1988. Palestinian boys near Manger Square.

(bottom)   Jerusalem, December 1988. A Palestinian student is arrested during clash.

■ p. 51   (top, left)   Sa'ir, December 1988. A *kaffiyah*-masked youngster leads a demonstration through the streets.

(top, right)   Khan Yunis refugee camp. April 1988. A girl encourages her little brother not to be afraid of the American visitors.

(bottom)	Beit Sahour, October 1988. The family of the town's latest young martyr at Mass at the Greek Orthodox Church.

■ pp. 80 & 81   Al-Ittihad Hospital, Nablus, October 18, 1988. The bleeding body of a child was rushed into the operating room while Phyllis Bennis and a Palestinian journalist were waiting for surgeons to remove a plastic bullet from Neal Cassidy's leg. Both Bennis and the journalist ran to grab one of Neal's cameras. It is unknown which of them snapped this photograph. Six hours of intensive medical care passed before the child died. His name was Zia Jihad Fayez Haj-Muhammad. He was 5 years old. This volume is dedicated to him.

■ p. 85   (top)   Jabaliya refugee camp, December 1988. Israeli troops on patrol among the camp's Palestinian population.

        (bottom)   Jerusalem, December 1988. Palestinian being questioned by Israeli Border Guards.

■ p. 86   (top)   Jerusalem, December 1988. Border Guards detain girl following clash.

        (bottom)   Bethlehem, November 1988. Soldiers patrol shopping district during strike hours.

■ p. 91   (top)   Jerusalem, October 1988. Soldiers atop the Damascus Gate monitor Arab Quarter of the Old City.

        (bottom)   Dheisha refugee camp, November 1988. Children standing at the doorstep of their home.

■ p. 92   (top)   Khan Yunis refugee camp, April 1988. A house was demolished by Israeli soldiers because the family did not have a permit for the roof extension they built for food storage.

    (bottom, left)   Deir Ammar, April 1988. The tear gas cannister reads "Federal Laboratories, Salzburg, Pennsylvania. Do not use in enclosed space." It was fired directly into the woman's home.

    (bottom, right)   Bani Na'im, October 1988. A woman who had stepped outside her door during a curfew had her leg broken by a large rock thrown at it by an Israeli soldier.

	(bottom)	Jerusalem, April 1988. Two Israeli soldiers sit guard outside a small shop in the Old City.

■ p. 115   (top)   Al-Bireh, October 1988. Women of families whose wage-earners are in prison, wounded or killed by Israelis, picking up relief checks from In'ash Al-Usra.

                          (bottom)   Kufr Na'meh, October 1988. A young clerk in the cooperative shop.

■ p. 118   (top)   Beita, November 1988. A woman laments to the sky at the funeral of a young martyr.

                          (bottom)   Yatta, December 1988. Palestinian youths.

■ p. 120 & 121   Sa'ir, November 1988. *Debka* dancers are part of a village-wide mobilization celebrating the declaration of Palestinian independence.

■ p. 123   (top)   Yatta, December 1988. Palestine's flags lead the march commemorating the first year of the intifada.

                          (bottom)   Algiers, November 1988. PLO Chairman Yasir Arafat during 19th session of Palestine National Council.

■ p. 124   (top)   Algiers, November 1988. The sign reads: "19th Session Palestine National Council, November 12–15, 1988, dedicated to the Intifada and Abu Jihad." Arafat is joined by Umm Jihad, widow of the slain leader, killed by Israeli commandos in April 1988.

■ p. 136 & 137   Ramallah, December 1988. A children's demonstration celebrates the first anniversary of the intifada.

■ p. 138   Sa'ir, November 1988. A boy celebrating the declaration of the new Palestinian state reaches to place his country's flag atop the highest point in the village.

The Authors

Phyllis Bennis is the United Nations correspondent for *Frontline* newspaper. She hosts "Frontlines: Middle East" on WBAI radio in New York, and is the Middle East correspondent for the award-winning radio series "Contragate/Undercurrents." She lives in Brooklyn, New York.

Neal Cassidy is a staff photographer for *Frontline* newspaper and Impact Visuals photo agency in New York. He has had several exhibitions of his photographs in the San Francisco Bay Area. He lives in Oakland, California.